ROOTS OF INSURGENCY IN NORTHEAST INDIA

ROOTS OF INSURGENCY IN NORTHEAST INDIA

Edited by
J B Bhattacharjee

AKANSHA PUBLISHING HOUSE
NEW DELHI-110002 (INDIA)

AKANSHA PUBLISHING HOUSE
4649-B/21, Ansari Road
Darya Ganj, New Delhi - 110 002
Ph.: 23263193/9811582579
Fax: 011-23263193
Email: ektabooks@yahoo.com

Roots of Insurgency in Northeast India

First Published 2007

ISBN 978–81–8370–138-9

PRINTED IN INDIA

Published by Akansha Publishing House, New Delhi and Printed at Aryan Enterprises, Delhi.

CONTENTS

PREFACE

The peoples in the north-eastern states of India are living in a state of turmoil caused by insurgency, militancy and movements of different types in various parts of the region for almost half a century. The civil society, which silently suffered the turmoil for a long time for various reasons, is now increasingly getting vocal in demanding that the state of turmoil must end and peace must dawn in the region. In some cases the well-meaning individuals and organizations volunteered to initiate dialogue with the activists for peaceful settlements of the outstanding problems. The emerging scenario demands that the intellectuals of the region should continue to contribute their share to the peace processes academically as a social responsibility. However, the success of the peace efforts would depend on a clear understanding of the root causes of the turmoil. Needless to say, these causes are expected to be identified accurately and impartially only by the academia. This publication is an effort in this direction.

The book emerges from a brainstorming session on 'Roots of Insurgency in Northeast India', organized by the Shillong Centre of the Institute of Northeast India Studies, in collaboration with the Women's College, Shillong, on 26th August 2006. The session was planned in two parts, viz. presentations and interactions. The forenoon was devoted to presentations, in which eight presenters made their submissions. The presentations were in the oral mode - in the form of extempore, although the presenters used their notes and data in course of the deliberations. These were voice-recorded and the transcripts were made available to the presenters for preparation of the drafts for publication. The afternoon session was devoted to interactions in which a good number of participants opened themselves up in frankly sharing their personal views on the roots of insurgencies and militancies in the region, with or without reference to the presentations made in the forenoon. The entire discourse was voice-recorded and the rapporteur could compare her own copious notes of the proceedings with the recorded version for preparation of the Postscript. The methodology adopted in conducting the brainstorming session and for preparation of the manuscript might explain why the publication took almost a year.

We expect the book to be useful to all those who are involved in the peace processes in Northeast India because we sincerely believe that no problem can be solved without understanding the root causes of the problem. The discourse convinced us that there is nothing like a north-eastern insurgency, and that there are several autonomous or isolated insurgencies, militancies and other movements in different parts and ethnic areas of the region which have over the years created an atmosphere of turmoil or an insurgent situation for the entire region. The roots of the problems vary from secessionism to demands for state or sub-state within India, or regional autonomy for ethnic areas within the states, or protection of ethnic and cultural identities. The economic and infrastructural backwardness, unemployment and lack of opportunities seemed to be common causes in almost all cases of insurgency and militancy. Peace can dawn only when the roots of turmoil are all uprooted. We shall consider our efforts rewarded if the book can make even a small contribution to the peace process.

Institute of Northeast India Studies deeply appreciates the support received from various quarters in organizing the brainstorming session and in publishing the proceedings in a book form. The initiative for the brainstorming session was entirely from the Shillong Centre of the Institute. Professor D R Syiemlieh, Chairman, Shillong Centre, took keen interest in the programme and did all the ground work for the success of the brainstorming session, although he could not personally attend in the session due to a very important meeting in Delhi on the same date. Shri Debasish Choudhury, Principal, Women's College, Shillong, and his colleagues and staff, provided the space and looked after all the logistics for the brainstorming session. The ICSSR-NERC, Shillong, participated in the effort through a financial support, while Dr C J Thomas, Director, ICSSR-NERC, himself an author of some important publications on insurgency, personally took keen interest in its academic contents. The high academic standard of the discourse was possible only due to the presenters and the participants. They braved the sensitivity of the subject and offered their balanced and impartial views in true academic spirit. Professor L S Gassah, a distinguished Political Scientist of the region, who chaired the brainstorming session, made the discourse absorbingly interesting by his timely interventions and moderations and by his own contributions. The media, the regional press and the local station of the Doordarshan in Shillong, joined the effort by extensively covering the event. A good number of my former colleagues and students in various places in the Northeast talked to me over telephone after reading about the brainstorming session in the newspapers or watching the television informing that they appreciated the initiative very much and that they would also like to participate if such programmes are organized in future, perhaps without knowing how encouraging were those calls to me and my colleagues in the Institute of Northeast India Studies. Finally, it is Akansha Publishing House, New Delhi, which has been specializing in publishing on the Northeast, came forward to complete the grand finality. In fact, Shri M P Misra, the enterprising proprietor of the House, took interest in the output of the brainstorming session no sooner had the event been over and wheeled speed in the work of the editor by reminding about it from time to time. I am in deed impressed by his love and concern for the Northeast.

Institute of Northeast India Studies
Kolkata - 700129
June 15, 2007

J B Bhattacharjee

PROPOSITIONS

KEYNOTE

—J B Bhattacharjee

Northeast India has been passing through insurgencies and militancies of various types for almost fifty years. Beginning in the Naga Hills in 1950s, an insurgent situation gradually spread to various other parts of the region. The number of outfits multiplied over the years, each one with own agenda. The originals broke into new outfits adding to the number, and in course of time, the splinters outnumbered the parent groups. The agenda in all cases are not necessarily challenging the Indian state or a demand for independent or sovereign state, as they include a host of other irreconcilables that range from local autonomy, or protection of cultural identity and economic and political interests, to the expulsion of the outsiders and ensuring that the land and resources in each ethnic area are exclusive preserves of the local community. The latest addition in the motive forces behind the turmoil is perhaps the financial extortion. In some parts of the region, where ethnicity is not a factor, the extortionist onslaught has proved to be the most tormenting. Although all those varieties would not technically satisfy the definitional requirement of an insurgency, each one is popularly identified as 'insurgent' or 'militant' and this has been helping the fictitious groups in creating an environment of panic and lawlessness to flourish in the region. Nevertheless, the Naga case and a few others (including the Mizo at a point of time) are clearly insurgencies in objectives and methods. The failure of the Indian state to politically tackle the problem at initial stages and to eliminate the conditions for the new demands and groups to emerge is believed to be the justifiable reason for the multiplicity and sustenance of the menace that the region has already suffered for such a long time. The cost of insurgency has proved to be very high, not only for the people of the region but the entire country. The situation has become so tormenting that the silent and the peace-loving majority is also gradually becoming vocal in demanding that the things cannot be allowed to continue for all time to come and a solution must be urgently found. However, a solution is possible only when the roots of the problem are identified and eliminated. This brainstorming session has been organized by the Institute of Northeast India Studies, through its Shillong Centre, as a response of the academia to its social responsibility to help the society and the political authority in resolving such issues in larger national and social interests. The objective is to find out at what point of time, where and under what conditions, the insurgency dawned in the region, and what are the factors that sustained the insurgency and promoted it for such a long time. In other words, why insurgency; where are its roots ? We are aware that terrorism or militancy is a global phenomenon today, but we are limiting ourselves to Northeast India, i.e. the region of our immediate concern, to identify the roots that are specific to this region. However, it does not deter us from looking into those factors which might have originated outside the region but influenced the growth of insurgencies here.

Before we proceed to address the key issues, it may be necessary to clarify that we are aware that 'insurgency', 'militancy', 'secessionism', 'terrorism', 'cross-border terrorism' – each of these terms have different connotations, definitions and meanings, but for our purpose here we can take them as one in so far as the basic features and the social consequences remain the same, viz. causing violence, threat of violence and a sense of insecurity in the minds of the citizens. Secondly, we are also aware that there is nothing like one insurgency in the Northeast. In fact, different groups and outfits are working in different states, or more precisely, in different ethnic and linguistic areas within the same state or in more than one adjoining states, with different agenda or mission, and without any common organizational frame or connectivity between themselves. The causes of insurgency or turmoil in different areas within the region are different and in many cases, the groups clashed with each other on the ground of conflicting objectives and interests. The methods and channels of operation are also different for different groups. More importantly, each outfit is autonomous, and fighting its own cause. Yet, we preferred to call it 'Insurgency in Northeast India' because all these 'insurgencies' and 'militancies' have created an 'insurgent situation' for the entire region with common fall-out and ramifications for the common people of the region. The fictitious and self-seeking groups are only taking advantage of the prevailing situation of lawlessness. The ground reality is that everything in the Northeast today goes in the name of insurgency. In short, we are using 'insurgency' in a collective singular sense and referring to the prevailing situation that is affronting the peace-loving masses.

The reason why we thought an intellectual discourse of this nature is necessary is that we come across so many publications, including seminar proceedings, addressed to various aspects of insurgency and terrorism, but 'why insurgency in Northeast India ?' does not become very clear from these publications. Recently, 'conflict resolution' became a very popular theme for seminars, but there too the emphasis is more on 'resolution' than on the 'causes' of the conflicts. Even the government, at times, wanted to solve the problem by various methods, which ranged from hard military actions like counter insurgency and unified command to the soft approaches of signing the accords and pumping in money, without identifying the causes of the problem. It may not be wrong to say that these efforts are something like treating the patient without diagnosing the decease. In our opinion, to find a solution to any problem, the causes or roots of the problem should be identified first. Therefore, today we are concentrating only on the 'Roots' of Insurgency in Northeast India.

In any effort to spot the roots of insurgency, it may be necessary to begin with the historical, geographical and anthropological factors of insurgency and the historical background of the insurgency itself. The geographical and historical isolation of the North-Eastern Region till the British colonial intervention was indeed phenomenal. It was so spectacular that the early state and polity formation processes in the region did not generally go beyond small geographical areas and ethnic boundaries, and in cases where it happened, the distinctions between the ethnic divisions were carefully maintained. In most cases, the polities were limited to village and clan level tribal formations. The spoken languages (mostly dialects) were too many and the absence of link languages, beyond the immediate borders, was deterrent to larger social and economic relationships. The interactions were limited to contiguous areas and around the markets; the villages and communities playing the role of trade buffer in respect of those beyond them. The raids and ambushes, head-hunting, inter-clannish feuds, inter- and intratribal warfare involving various forms of violence compelled the tribes and communities to maintain distance from each other, while the Mughal invasions in the mediaeval period, and thereafter the Burmese and the British interventions in 18th-19th century, created almost an universal psyche that was prone to easily accepting the existence of so many powerful enemies beyond the region. A sense of exclusiveness and mutual distrust, particularly about the outsiders, might be the result of historical experience of immigration, exploitation and deprivation in the past. It may also be interesting to examine whether the traditions like head-hunting involving raids, surprise and ambuscades, or human sacrifices in some of the temples, are in some way linked to the cruelty perpetrated in some of the extremists' onslaughts.

The British colonialization, which had in fact for the first time in history integrated the Northeast in a single political system in the subcontinent, namely, the British Indian colonial state, further promoted and legitimized the isolation within the region by its segregating policies that created blocks and barriers, particularly in the hill region, and infused a hills-plains divide. On the other hand, the early British expansionist endeavours found stiff resistance from the hill tribes and the sporadic armed revolts continued in some areas, in some form or other, from time to time, till the end of the British rule. These revolts may be good enough examples to suggest that the hill people could not reconcile with the loss of their independence to the alien British rulers. Nonetheless, the historic Indian national movement could not make any significant impact in the hill areas. On the contrary, the demand for independence of the ethnic groups could be heard in some areas at the time of the transfer of power. The Naga case is an example. In the Mizo Hills also the opinion was divided. In Manipur, there was strong resistance from certain quarters to joining the Indian Union under the Instrument of Accession.

The colonial reorganization of Bengal and Assam (1826, 1874, 1905 & 1911) had already created conditions for social tension and social conflicts in the post-colonial phase. When the Ahom Kingdom or the Assamese heartland was annexed in 1826 it was made an administrative division under a Commissioner within Bengal, and thereafter the neighbouring hill areas were taken over in installments and made parts of the Assam Division, except the Garo Hills, which was included in the Cooch Behar Division, and the South Lushai (Mizo) Hills, which was in Chittagong Division. In 1874 Assam Division (including the hill districts) was separated from Bengal and made a Chief Commissioner's Province, and three Bengal districts (namely, Cachar and Sylhet from the Dacca Division and Goalpara from the Cooch Behar Division), with a large indigenous Bengali population, were transferred to Assam to make the new province 'viable'. The Garo Hills and the Lushai Hills were also transferred to this new province. The creation of this multi-ethnic and multi-lingual province, in which the traditional Assamese area and population formed a minor segment, created the initial conditions for future conflicts. In

1905 Bengal was partitioned again and a province called 'Eastern Bengal and Assam' was created with Dhaka (Dacca) as the headquarters. This new province included the erstwhile Chief Commissioner's province of Assam and the eastern districts of Bengal. The Assamese and the tribal communities formed small minorities in this large Bengali dominated province. This period also saw the large-scale immigration of Muslim peasants from Eastern Bengal into the Brahmaputra Valley at official encouragement and patronage, and the process, called 'colonization scheme', continued even after the partition was annulled in 1911 and Assam reverted to its earlier size and status as a Chief Commissioner's province. This 'British Assam' still included the hill areas (Khasi-Jaintia, Garo, North Cachar or Dimasa, Karbi or Mikir, Naga and Mizo or Lushai hills) and three traditional Bengali districts (Cachar, Sylhet and Goalpara). As a mater of fact, by creating a multi-ethnic and multilingual province in which the traditional Assamese area and the Assamese population formed only a minority, and yet by naming it 'Assam', the British colonialists planted the seeds of future discord, and this may be seen as an important root of insurgency in the post-colonial period.

After the independence of India in 1947, the 'assimilation' policy of the Government of Assam to make Assamese the official language saw the alienation of the non-Assamese population and large-scale violence in the Brahmaputra Valley in 1960-61. This also witnessed the beginning of the movement for hill states which ultimately resulted in the reorganizations of Assam. The process does not seem to be over as the demands for more states are continuing. The Government of India proved itself always very slow in responding to the problems of the ethnic and linguistic minorities, who had to protect themselves and to defend their rights and interests against the dominant group that enjoyed the support of the state authority. It may not be wrong to say that in those cases the fear of domination and loss of ethnic, linguistic and cultural identity led to resistance and resistance led to militancy.

On the other hand, the large presence of a non-local or non-indigenous population, which was tending to become domiciled, - sharing resources and emerging as pressure groups in the democratic polity, was another irritant which resulted in several instances of riots and violence in 1950s and 60s. The slow pace of development, despite the resource abundance of the region, and the intellectuals squarely holding the central government or the Indian state responsible for the economic backwardness of the region in 1960s and 70s, also contributed its share in surcharging the public opinion. The educated unemployed and under-employed youths were most visibly aggrieved and they suffered frustration and disappointment. The 1960s and 70s witnessed the emergences of a large number of regional political parties with regional agenda. These regional political parties championed the issues of economic backwardness, protection of rights and interests of the locals ('indigenous people', 'sons of the soil', etc) and the exploitation by the outsiders. A battle line was gradually drawn between 'we' and 'they'.

The anti-foreigners movements in 1970s and 80s, though peaceful and democratic in contents, were coupled with mutual distrust, social alienation and sporadic violence in Assam, Tripura and Meghalaya. In Assam – the heartland of the movement - the movement was professedly directed against the illegal migrants from Bangladesh and Nepal, but rhetoric of the movement created a sense of insecurity in the minds of genuine citizens who are from other regions of the country, particularly the Bengalis who are either indigenous in parts of this region or domiciled for two to three generations. In Tripura, the cry against the alarming growth of non-tribal population culminated in the Mandai massacre, emergence of radical tribal political groups, and ultimately, the armed militancy. The economic grievances were voiced in various forms during this period, particularly in Assam, Meghalaya, Manipur and Tripura. The oil blockade in Assam is an example. The accords, which were signed during the course of the movements and after, contained specific provisions for economic development, but most of those promises remained unfulfilled. The Bodoland Movement in Lower and Central Assam and the ASDC Movement in Karbi Anglong-North Cachar Hills gained momentum during the Assam Movement.

To put in a historical sequence, the insurgency in the Northeast first surfaced in the Naga Hills in 1950s, followed by the Mizo Hills (60s) and Manipur (early-70s), with secessionist agendas. The militant outfits emerged in Assam, Tripura and Meghalaya during the years of the Assam Movement (late-70s & early-80s) and the number of outfits increased in the later years (1980s & 90s). The United Liberation Front of Assam (ULFA) and the Tripura National Volunteers (TNV) became major players in the Brahmaputra Valley of Assam and Tripura respectively. The Hynniewtrep National Liberation Council (HNLC) and the Achik National Volunteers Council (ANVC) are active in the Khasi-Jaintia and the Garo hills segments respectively of Meghalaya. The insurgents' presence is heard from Arunachal Pradesh as well.

In Manipur initially only one group spearheaded the insurgent activities, but in course of time the number increased by breaking away from the parent groups and the emergence of new outfits. In Tripura, the number is as large as that of the tribes in the state and in the dominant Tripuri group also there are break-away groups and factions. In Assam, the ULFA showed the way, but today there are Karbi, Dimasa, Bodo and other militants. Some tribal and non-tribal outfits are working in the Karbi and Bodo inhabited areas. The Dima Halam Daoga (DHD) is active in the North Cachar Hills and its cadres have been extending their operations from time to time to the neighbouring Barak Valley. The situation has in deed been complicated by the multiplicity of the outfits within the same ethnic areas through divisions in the original groups and the splinters indulging in mutual conflicts and clashes and internecine warfare. A recent media report informed the emergence of new outfits in the two hill districts of Assam, called the 'Karbi Longri N C Hills Liberation Front' and the 'United People's Democratic Solidarity', while the 'Black Window' is a new faction of the DHD. The Black Window is said to be active in the bordering areas of the Barak Valley. The same media also informed that a new militant group, called the United Democratic Liberation Army (UDLA), has started operating in the Barak Valley districts of Karimganj and Hailakandi. The group has already masterminded at least four kidnappings in the Hailakandi district during May-August 2006. It is extorting money from the farmers, traders, teachers and government officials in rural areas in those two districts. The outfit first attracted public attention in July 2006 when it abducted eight farmers from a village under Katlicherra block in Hailakandi district. The captives could be freed after eight days when the CRPF and the Assam Armed Police Battalion launched an extensive raid in the jungles of Katlicherra block on the Assam-Mizoram border. The report says that the UDLA is being led by a Reang duo (S Moni and Manaraj Reang, aged 30 and 28 respectively) and this small group comprises of only 30 members and possesses some SLRs and only one AK-47 assault rifle. The same report stated that another militant group, called the United Liberation Front of Barak Valley has recently started operating in the Karimganj district. Led by one P Apeto, this group draws its cadres from the Reangs and the Bengali Muslims. These two outfits came up when the powerful Barak Valley Youth Liberation Force, led by Parameshwar Reang, was fighting a losing battle against the paramilitary forces and was rocked by internecine quarrels amongst its own cadres. The Barak Valley is otherwise a peaceful area. Only some extortionist outfits, particularly those belonging to the Reang tribe, have been occasionally involved in kidnapping officials and businessmen to earn ransom. Several cases of abductions of the tea garden officials and businessmen in the Lakhipur area of Cachar district were reported in past few years. The leaders and cadres of the outfits operating the Barak Valley are generally from the neighbouring areas, besides a small number of Reang villages in the remote part of the Hailakandi district. In fact, the Barak Valley scenario is an important example of how the criminal gangs are taking advantage of the prevailing insurgent situation in other parts of the region for the purpose of robbery and dacoity and to what levels the high ideals of insurgency or militancy can degenerate. The presence of the extortionist outfits, which use the militant names and collect ransom by using militants' method, is heard almost from all parts of the region. As a matter of fact, the extortions in some forms is resorted to even by the genuinely insurgent and militant groups, who have been collecting funds by sending 'demand notes' to rich people and by imposing 'taxes' on the common people to finance their activities.

Another dimension of the insurgent activities, which should not be missed, is the cross-border movements of the militants. Since the problem started in the Naga Hills in 1950s some unfriendly neighbouring countries had been providing the militants food and shelter and safe passage, and even arms and training, which encouraged and promoted the insurgent activities in the Northeast. The reports of training camps for the Northeast militants in China, Burma (Myanmar), East Pakistan (now, Bangladesh) and Bhutan poured in through media almost since the beginning of the insurgency in the region. The militants are also known to be using sophisticated imported weapons in various actions and encounters. These facts clearly reflect on the role of some foreign countries in insurgency or militancy in Northeast India. It is possible that some of these countries, who are India's immediate neighbours and directly border the North-Eastern Region, were actually responsible for instigating some of the ethnic groups to rise against the new-born Indian state to weaken its nation-building processes and economic development. At least, there can be no denying of the fact that the insurgency, which began with one or two ethnic groups, grew step by step over the years by attracting more and more groups and areas and it could continue for such a long time mainly due to external support. This 'external root' of insurgency deserves serious consideration. Nonetheless, this dimension of the problem does not augur well with the articulation of a 'good neighbourly' foreign policy of the Indian state. This is in deed very disappointing when we recall the dream of 'a comity of nations' and 'peaceful coexistence' of our national leaders on the eve of India's independence (Tagore's 'global village' and Nehru's "*panch-sheel*', are examples). A section of the leaders even talked of a just deal to the neighbours and the South Asian solidarity. One of them, Sarat Chandra Bose went to the extent of proposing a 'United State of South Asia" (USSA) with complete autonomy and internal freedom for the federating units as a new model of federations. Nehru's slogan was "*Hindi-Chini Bhai Bhai*'. The ground reality is that Pakistan was born as a 'hostile neighbour' with an eye on Kashmir, while the McMahon Line was an irritation for China. The Nehruvian era could not sort out the outstanding issues with China and Pakistan. China invaded India in 1962, while the year 1965 is remembered for the Indo-Pak War. These dates are also important in the history of insurgencies in Naga Hills, Mizo Hills and Manipur. The unfriendly neighbours, it seems, had been successful thereafter in pushing the border wars into India's own soil to be fought with its own people. Despite India's help for liberation of Bangladesh, the ULFA and many other outfits had no problem in getting shelter and running training camps in that erstwhile eastern wing of Pakistan. The camps sprouted in Bhutan also, and the militants had to be flashed out in an Indo-Bhutanese joint operation only three years ago. All these provide a sad profile of India's foreign policy, particularly towards the neighbouring countries, and this failure may also be attributed as a factor for the rise and growth of insurgency or cross-border terrorism in Northeast India which has a more than four thousand two hundred kilometers of porous international border and is linked with the rest of the country by the less than twenty-five kilometers 'Siliguri neck'.

The domestic policy of the Indian state was no better a success than the foreign policy in so far as the insurgency is concerned. It is said that the government could do well to pacify the handful of insurgents at the initial stages, rather than antagonizing them by hard words and encouraging by soft actions. It is also believed that had the Government of Assam been fair in its policies towards the ethnic minorities the things could be different. Many in the region today recall how the administra-tion ridiculed itself on those occasions. The senior officers in administration and the men in army were almost all of them from outside the region and their knowledge in history, geography, society and culture of the people of the region was very poor. It is believed that they could at least alienate the insurgents from the rest of the society and tackle the problem more effectively. The effort of the administration is said to have fallen much short of what was expected. On the contrary, the indiscriminate harassment and the ruthless torture and killing of the innocent people strengthened the determination of the insurgents. The stories of administrative excesses and the highhandedness of the police and army personnel, including the molestation of young women, spread like wildfire, which provoked the youths to join the ranks of the insurgents in large numbers. The insurgents also gradually earned the support and sympathy of the community for the same reasons. This explains how the insurgency in some areas succeeded in assuming a mass character, at least for sometimes, and it could spread from area to area or community to community, although the roots and circumstances for each could be different. Therefore, the violation of human rights and the administrative excesses and highhandedness of the police and military personnel should be considered among the roots of the later phases of insurgencies and the growth and sustenance of the earlier ones.

Much before the insurgency broke out in the region in 1970s on a larger scale, the people, particularly the politicians and the intellectuals had been complaining of economic backwardness of the region. They could see that roads and the railway net-work had remained almost the same as they were laid by the British without any improvement for many years, while agriculture suffered stagnation and deterioration without any modernization; not a single dam was constructed, not even one major irrigation project taken up, and no industry worth the name was being established. The conditions of some of the major internal roads were worse than what these were in the British time, and the once flourishing tea industry was fast getting exhausted. None of the infrastructure required for economic growth was developed in the region. On the other hand, the raw-materials were taken out of the region for processing in various factories, and the two major rivers – the Brahmaputra and the Barak - were creating flood havoc every year. Those who visited other parts of the country and important cities for various purposes could see that the development was taking place in those areas in much faster speed than in the Northeast. They could know through radio and newspapers the claims of the central ministers and leaders that the country was progressing well. The intellectuals in the region highlighted the potential of the Northeast to progress on the basis of its own natural resources and the manpower, while the politicians began to blame the central government squarely for the indifference and step-motherly attitude to the Northeast. These issues were systematically highlighted through media during the years of the Assam Movement and became popular themes of household discussions. The elders reminded the new generation that during the Chinese invasion in 1962 how the then Prime Minister, Jawaharlal Nehru, on a rumour that the Chinese had reached Tezpur, had exclaimed, "My heart goes for the people of Assam". This and several other similar anecdotes went round the press, platform and popular gossips in the buses, streets, tea-stalls and drawing rooms to bring home the point that the Government of India had 'no love lost' for Assam or the Northeast. No wonder, the insurgents in early stages enjoyed silent support and sympathy from the respective communities. They were looked upon as heroes, patriots and messiahs, who were braving the odds and gallows of the administration for the salvation of the community. The policy of the central government changed sharply in 1980s when they began to sign accords after accords with the various agitating groups promising economic development and solutions of the vexed problems, and in 1990s they began generously to pump in money through special schemes and packages for the economic development of the North-Eastern States. The government asked all the central ministries to spend at least 10% of their budget on the Northeast, revamped the North-Eastern Council (NEC), and finally, created a separate ministry for the Development of the North-Eastern Region (DONER). By then the insurgency had already reached almost all parts of the Northeast, either directly or indirectly. Besides the fact that it is too late a policy decision to prove genuine concern for the Northeast, it sent a wrong signal to the insurgents and the politicians as the weakness of the central government. Many took it as a success of the militancy, and some of the ethnic areas which had not opted for the insurgents' way so far, now regretted not getting a due share of the liberal funding. Some insurgents (no matter, fake or genuine) began to surrender in groups, and the state governments were justified in asking funds separately for the rehabilitation of the 'surrendered militants'. One is not sure, whether the funds received for containing militancy are not utilized for other purposes. A condition was thus created for a politician-militant nexus to grow for endurance of the flow of funds. Many in the region do believe that had the Government of India given due attention to the development of the region since independence of the country, and enforced accountability and ensured proper utilization of funds, the region would not have been taken over by the insurgents and militants for such a long time.

It must, however, be appreciated that in one area, despite the 'negligence' or 'indifference' of the authority that be, the Northeast made spectacular strides, and that is, education, including higher and technical education. Some good schools and colleges were established in this region during the British period, particularly by the Christian missionaries, and the first university, namely, the Gauhati University, was established in 1948. A large number of schools and colleges, and also few more universities, have come up since then. Today, there are as many as twelve universities, including two agricultural universities, besides the Deemed universities like NIT at Silchar, IIT at Guwahati and NERIST at Itanagar. There are at least four engineering colleges, five medical colleges and three colleges of nursing in the public sector. The medium of instructions generally continued to be English; in the hill areas it is only English. There are about five hundred general degree and junior colleges, most of which were established through private initiative. The literacy rate is higher than the national average. This could be an advantage of the region over the others. However, the Assam Movement in the Brahmaputra Valley and the associated or parallel movements in other parts of Assam and the region for sometimes affected the academic life in 1970s and early 80s. Nevertheless, the things returned to normalcy within few years. The campus unrest is in deed very rare in this region.

A spectacular weakness in the field of education, however, was the fact that the courses offered in various streams were generally traditional or conventional in nature and no serious attempt was made till 1990s for introduction of professional and vocational courses or to establish industry-university tie-ups for the employment of the products. The things have improved to some extent in the recent years with the introduction of professional course in some of the universities in the region and establishment of some private professional institutes and private medical and engineering colleges. Some of these private institutions are affiliated to universities in the region, while others are running the courses and programmes on behalf of institutes and universities elsewhere and some are working even through the distance mode. The public sector professional institutes are also coming up gradually, and the establishment of the North-Eastern Indira Gandhi Regional Institute of Health and Medical Sciences (NEIGRIHMS), an Indian Institute of Management (IIM) and Institute of Food and Nutrition and Catering Technology (IFNCT) at Shillong are very good examples of the new dispensation. Nevertheless, the industry-institute linkages for employment remains a distant dream as such industries are still rare in the Northeast.

Unfortunately, the progress of education, which could decidedly be an advantage of the region, proved to be a serious cause of growing unemployment problem, and it became one of the major factors which promoted insurgency in the region. The universities and other institutions went on producing thousands of graduates in various streams every year, but the state and the society failed to employ them. The employment opportunity for the white color job seekers in the region was limited to the government service and teaching in private or public educational institutions only. Within few years of independence the scope in this sector also became dry, as the governments in the states and the central organizations could not create new jobs after a point and eventually imposed a virtual ban on recruitments, and eventually, even ordered withdrawal of the vacant posts. The public sector in this region has always been very small, and the private sector worth the name hardly exists. That the industries did not grow in the region was the main reason for the lack of job opportunities. By 1960s the unemployment had already become a serious problem in the Northeast, and in spite of this resounding unemployment problem, in the years after 1970, more colleges and universities were established. In fact, the 1960s and 70s witnessed a mushrooming of schools and colleges in the region. The result was that every year several thousands of youths were added to the educated jobless category. The youths suffered frustrations and disappointments and they were looking for alternatives. It is a well known fact that this educated unemployed category filled the ranks of the militants in 1970s and 80s. They also launched new outfits in new areas, including the pseudo groups for the purpose of extortions only. The militancy created not only job opportunity but also fetched big income. The cry was that the higher and technical education which fails to ensure job is meaningless. The frustration percolated downwards; the drop-outs increased in colleges and high schools and many of these drop-outs swelled the ranks of the militants (genuine or pseudo). What is generally heard is that the educated unemployed and drop-outs are more in the extortionist groups. They have nothing to do with the insurgents' agenda of autonomy or liberation, although they give themselves militants' names, including 'liberation army', 'tigers' and so on, use only toy pistols and the like, and involve themselves in abductions and thereafter, in demanding ransoms. They take up this career as an alternative to employment, but they can earn more money than what any employment can offer them. The genuine insurgents are of course different; they have clear agenda and certain principles to follow. Right or wrong, they have a mission to fulfill. Nonetheless, there must be many among the recruits in the ranks of the insurgents, who were frustrated and demoralized by prolonged unemployment after they had completed their education, and it is frustration and anger that impelled them to join the ranks of the insurgents or militants. The governments either in the states or at the centre did nothing to address the unemployment problem or to redress the frustration and disappointment of the youths. Therefore, it can hardly be denied that the educated unemployment problem in the region contributed significantly to the growth of insurgency or militancy. This may not be a root factor, but it is certainly one of the key factors which promoted and sustained insurgency (or militancy) in Northeast India.

It may also not be possible to separate the problem of insurgency from the question of ethnicity in Northeast India. In fact, the ethnic polarization in the region began in 1960 when the Assam Official Language Act (1960) sought to make Assamese the only official language of the state. The policy was opposed by the non-Assamese, particularly the Bengalis who constituted the second largest linguistic group in the state and more than eighty-five percent of the total population in the Barak Valley. The All-Assam Non-Assamese Convention, held in Silchar in July 1960, was attended by the important hill leaders from Khasi, Garo and Mizo hills and some plains tribal leaders from the Brahmaputra Valley. In the meantime, the language riots were reported from many areas in the Brahmaputra Valley. The amendment of the Act, at the intervention of the central government ('Shastri Formula' authored by the then Union Home Minister Lal Bahadur Shastri) to make provision for Bengali in the Barak Valley and English in the hill districts, did not fully satisfy the hill leaders, who wanted a long term guarantee to their ethnic identity which they realized would not be feasible within the state of Assam in the context of 'assimilation' (Assamese-ization ?) policy of its leaders. The Eastern India Tribal Union (EITU) championed the question of rights and interests of the tribals, while the All Party Hill Leaders Conference (APHLC) came into existence to fight for a hill state. In course of time, the hill state movements succeeded in the creation of Meghalaya and Mizoram by way of reorganization of Assam. The linguistic minorities still suffered a sense of insecurity in Assam. The polarization was more clearly manifested in 1972 when Assamese was sought to be made the only medium of instructions in the universities in Assam. Some Bodo, Dimasa and Bengali leaders took initiative in forming the Linguistic Minorities Rights Committee (LMRC), and they were joined by leaders of a number of linguistic groups in the Brahmaputra Valley. The Plains Tribal Council of Assam (PTCA) demanded a state for the plains tribals in the Brahmaputra Valley which eventually culminated in the prolonged Bodoland movement, while in the remaining two hill district in Assam (namely, Karbi Anglong and North Cachar Hills) movement started for an Autonomous State under the banner of the Autonomous State Demand Committee (ASDC). A section of the Ahoms also raised the demand for a separate state in Upper Assam. Some of the smaller ethnic groups in the Brahmaputra Valley, who were on the process of assimilation, reasserted their identity and raised demands for autonomous councils for the respective tribal blocks and villages. The Assam Movement (1979) was for the detection and deportation of the foreigners, but the participation of the ethnic and linguistic minorities was only marginal. It was in course of this movement, as already said, that several insurgent or militant groups surfaced in the region, including the United Liberation Front of Assam (ULFA). These facts make it clear that the assertion of ethnic identity became a fact of life in the region. The majority group tended to dominate the minority groups, while the minorities wanted the protection of their ethnic identity. In the process, the mutual suspicion and distrust dominated the relationship. The polarization process started in Assam with the 'assimilation' policy of a section of the Assamese leaders and intellectuals which put all other ethnic minorities on guard. Similarly, in Tripura, the tribal unrest centered on the question of Bengali domination and the fear of loss of tribal identity. The insurgent groups were formed on ethnic basis and their demands are also concerned with the respective ethnic groups only. When the Naga Hills district of Assam was converted into the state of

Nagaland, the Tuensang area (a Naga inhabited area) of the North-East Frontier Agency (NEFA, now called Arunachal Pradesh) was transferred to Nagaland. However, the Naga areas of Manipur remained in that state. The Naga insurgency took up the cause of all Nagas and the cadres were from all Naga areas, including those in Manipur. The Mizo insurgency championed the cause of the Mizos, and the non-Mizos had no place in the Mizo National Front (MNF). Similarly, insurgency in Manipur took up the cause of liberation of the Meiteis. Although the splinter groups emerged in later years, the Meitei character of the movement did not change. The Tripura National Volunteers (TNV) initially took up the cause of all tribes in Tripura, but ultimately it concerned itself to the Tripuris (Deb Barmans) only when the outfits gradually emerged from other tribes. The ULFA possibly included some Ahoms and plains tribals, but it is basically Assamese and limited to the cause of the Brahmaputra Valley alone. There are Bodo, Karbi, Dimasa, Bru and various other outfits who championed the interests of their respective ethnic groups only. The Khasi-Jaintias and the Garos participated unitedly in the APHLC Movement for the creation of Meghalaya, but the ethnic division - complaints of domination and deprivation – surfaced before long. Today, Hynniewtrep National Liberation Council (HNLC) is a Khasi-Jaintia outfit, while Achik National Volunteer Council (ANVC) is a Garo outfit. There is nothing like a north-eastern insurgency; the insurgents have never formed even a common front or raised a common demand for the region. Each group is fighting the cause of its own ethnic group. All these facts are related to the ethnic questions in the Northeast – domination of one group over the other and the fear of deprivation and loss of identity of the others. Therefore, the possibility of an ethnic root of the insurgency or militancy also should not be overlooked.

It may also be necessary to be inward-looking and resorting to self-introspection to understand whether or not some inner contradictions in the local societies are also facilitating the growth and sustenance of the insurgent situation in the region. The progress of education and the process of modernization sometimes effect the division of the traditional societies into forward and backward, articulate and the introvert, rich and the poor, etc. The advance section might have a tendency to monopolize the resources and opportunities, while the backward would feel marginalized, deprived and exploited. The value system or the moral standard may change for the affluent and the new rich, while the marginalized might still adhere to old values and traditions. Both the sections might experience some stratifications within own ranks and files. The forward section is more susceptible to vulnerability and moral degradation due to affluence and the ramifications of a new life-style. The flow of money and corruption at various levels are said to be splendid in the Northeast. The problem of frustration of the youths due to broken families, unattended adolescence and gender inequality are already worrying the intelligentsia in many societies. The instances of drug abuse and HIV/AIDS are also said to be on the increase. Therefore, it may be necessary to examine the possible impact of the social contradictions, particularly the loss of traditional social values, on the insurgent or militant situation in the region.

Finally, the formats and dimensions of insurgency and

militancy in the region are so many that the roots are also likely to be different in each specific case or group of cases. In the meantime, the number of the extortionist groups is also like to be very large. As a matter of fact, these fictitious groups might have already outnumbered the genuinely insurgent or militant groups who are fighting for the cause or causes they feel are genuine and what they stand for. Therefore, a study of the history of the origin and rise of each group involved in the turmoil is essential to understand what causes and issues it stands for. The motivation and the mode of operation of a group will determine its character and the nature of response or reaction it deserves from the state and society. By this method the fictitious or pseudo groups of extortionists can be first identified and dealt with under ordinary law for the criminal activities. But issues of the insurgents and the militants are political in nature and these can be settled only politically through negotiations in truly democratic spirit. It may be easy to dismiss the demands of the insurgents or militants by saying that they are all 'misguided youths', but this may not solve the problem of insurgency or end the sufferings of the silent masses. Any genuine effort to find a solution must start by spotting the roots of tensions and conflicts so that those roots can be eliminated and a civil society is allowed to dawn in the region.

PRESENTATIONS

1
PRESENTATION

—Binayak Dutta

The recent decades in the history of Northeast India have been gripped by one determining political phenomenon – i.e. insurgency. What comes at the fore of our deliberation today, to my mind, is : what is insurgency? Is insurgency an expression of suppressed voices ? Or, is insurgency a movement or protest against the state for non-fulfillment of a long pending demand? Or, is it a movement against the Indian state to carve out an independent country ? It may be important to underline in this context that the standard definitions of insurgency have tried to describe it as an armed insurrection or uprising against an established civil authority, while the persons engaging themselves in insurgency are called the 'insurgents'.

There is no doubt that the term 'insurgency' has come to symbolize a state of lawlessness and armed revolt against the state. The important element associated with the phenomenon is the fact that neither are the insurgents' organizations granted any formal recognition within the state structure, nor are their means of expression of dissent recognized as legal and legitimate. On the other hand, the insurgent bodies also do not recognize the state as in any way a lawfully constituted body; and hence, they have no hesitation in denying its legitimacy. Therefore, the entire process of an interaction between the two bodies is represented by mutual antagonism, or mutual violence. The moot point in this discourse is the question of 'legitimacy' and 'illegitimacy' of their mutually exclusive existence in the fabric of polity, except the occasional violent contacts and confrontations. But today in the contemporary world, insurgency has come to afflict almost every corner of the globe as an expression of dissent and protest. While in the context of the world scenario today the insurgency has come to become almost synonymous with any kind of a protest against the American-led multinational forces hegemony, in the Indian context it has become synonymous with any kind of an assertion of any ethnic group or tribe or community to register its demands or to make its voices heard and the counter-measures by the state to put down such voices. And in Northeast India, the people are living with insurgency for almost half a century. The ground reality in this region is that the strengths and assertions of insurgency are as varied as the targets of the insurgents themselves are. The ethnic groups are too many in this region, so is the number of the insurgent bodies. The conflicts started here in the form of domination of the smaller by the larger groups, and the small groups asserting their ethnic identities and demanding the protection of such identities. The established form of polity, namely, the democracy was not considered as sufficient for such protection, as the smaller groups had lesser or no representation in the constitutional authorities who could decide on the basis of a majority.

Another important element that comes to focus about insurgency is the use of terror as the dominant mode of its assertions or the dominant means of its existence. Hence, most of the insurgent groups have come out to negate the discursive mode of political settlement, or at least, to openly emphasize the futility of this method. The methods of the insurgents are, therefore, at direct variance with the philosophy of any kind of the liberal democratic political order, though their demands had often been to carve out a space for themselves in the liberal capitalist world order. Peace, which is the fundamental bedrock of the liberal capitalist socio-political system, is what is sought to be disrupted by the insurgents. In this sense, the role that the insurgents play is that of offering not only a critique of the liberal world order but in most occasions a challenge to its existence and the norms that it seeks to uphold. The mode of terror adopted by the insurgents, therefore, seeks to produce widespread fear in the minds of the people who are ordinary residents of the liberal democratic space and who participate in the state through the process of voting only. Hence expressions of popular will, or mandate, or support, are opposed by the insurgents as this is opposed to their existence and often are used to justify their unjustifiability. In this context, the efforts to observe certain days as special to the state are seen as an anathema to their existence and ideology. Some of the insurgent groups in the Northeast, therefore, for the past few years have been issuing calls for boycotting the 'Independence Day' (15th August) and the 'Republic Day' (26th January) celebrations, which are so sacrosanct to the Indian State and the Constitution of India. The insurgents' position here is perhaps that the participation in such celebrations would tantamount to the acceptance of the authority of the Indian State and the submission to its Constitution.

Insurgency, therefore, can be variously classified on the basis of their influence, organization, means of expression, ideology, and their structure. While in some cases ideology emerges as the most determining factor for the establishment of the insurgent body, in many other cases the area of their actual operation could also determine the nature of their demands and hence, their identity. It is a well known fact that in Northeast India all insurgent (or militant) groups are not necessarily anti-Indian or asking for sovereign states for themselves, as some them are the products of ethnic conflicts and wanted to protect the rights and interests of their respective communities. The time lost by the authority in responding to their demands, in some cases, might have effected changes in their position.

Another very important element of insurgency embedded in their anti-state character is the support that these insurgents receive from various organizations, and other external governments, which also shape the organization of the insurgent bodies. A classical case in point is the movement in the state of Jammu and Kashmir. Another problem that is evident in this entire discourse is the dilemma between the domains of claims and counter-claims of legitimacy of ideology and action of the state and the insurgents as the anti-state. The causes or roots of insurgency therefore can be traced to a variety of impetus. While some would claim ideological divergence with the dominant political philosophy of the state as evident in the conflict between the Islamic insurgents of Iraq and the Western

Liberal Government there, the others would merely look at insurgency from the stand point of protest being registered. In this second form, the insurgents have been pushed into this situation by the muted response of the state and its organs to the various demands raised by the society and polity that these insurgents stand to represent from time to time. The fact that some of the insurgent groups in the Northeast do enjoy the support from the neighbouring countries have been beyond any doubt, while there are also some instances of the civil society taking initiative for dialogues and negotiated settlements within the framework of the Constitution of India.

Yet another factor for insurgency seems to be a contest between the elite of the two contesting political and social domains. This position is also attributed to the perception that while the state does not listen, violence forces it to take notice and to negotiate. Another potent factor seems to be the projection by the insurgents of a better tomorrow, which contributes to the perception of the 'better tomorrow for which bloodshed today'. This endears the movement to a section of the civil society from which a part of the support base – financial or manpower – is drawn. It is possibly a combination of the ideological element and the civil society that grants to an insurgent movement its potency and provokes the state to negotiate with it. The recent trends in Northeast India have shown that there is a change in this relationship between the insurgent groups and the civil society, where the civil society which does not cooperate with the insurgents or sympathize with its ideology are seen as representatives of the state that these insurgents stand to oppose.

Finally, it is also a fact that insurgency is a potent means but rarely an end in itself which makes the phenomenon a complex one, and a relevant issue to deliberate. A pertinent point that could be related is the question of Human Rights becoming a cause and causality of insurgency itself. In this context the Human Rights question leads us into a viscous cycle of justifying excesses in the form of violence and counter-violence between the state and the counter-state. The importance of any exercise in understanding the phenomenon of insurgency can hardly be overemphasized. An analysis of the phenomenon, and the organization, ideology and expression of the insurgents, in other words, the rhetoric of insurgency, may help us identify the roots of the insurgency itself.

2

PRESENTATION

—H. Srikanth

Before one makes efforts to identify the roots of insurgency in Northeast India, it is essential to be clear as to what one should mean by the term, 'insurgency'. Should this expression be used to refer to all kinds of armed oppositions that are visible in the region or should one confine the term to only those organized secessionist movements which are targeting the Indian State with the avowed purpose of establishing their own sovereign states? Further, it may be useful to spell out whether we would like to describe all activities of different armed groups as insurgent activities, or use the idiom only to the activities of those groups which enjoy some amount of sympathy and support among large sections of people belonging to the communities that the groups claim to be representing. Answers to such questions are important, for the Indian Intelligence sources claim that more than one hundred militant groups are operating in Northeast India. But when start probing deep, one realizes that more than half the groups identified as militant are either insignificant or fictitious. Of the remaining, the groups like Adivasi Cobra Militant Force in Assam, United Bengali Liberation Front in Tripura, Bru

National Liberation Front (BNLF) in Mizoram etc., actually came into existence basically to protect their respective communities from the attacks of more powerful militant groups or communities in the region of their present habitation. Some like SULFA (euphemism for organized surrendered ULFA militants) are the creations of the governments, which wanted to use them against more powerful militant groups challenging their authority. Although some like Hynniewtrep National Liberation Council (HNLC), Achik National Volunteers Council (ANVC), Dima Halam Daoga (DHD), Zomi Revolutionary Army (ZRA), Kuki National Volunteers (KNV), etc., also talk of declared independence, yet they appear to be working more for greater autonomy or separate state status within the Indian Union. In fact, the Bodo Liberation Tigers (BLT) or Mizo National Front (MNF), which advocated secession initially, gave up their armed struggle and accepted greater autonomy or separate state status within the Indian Union. Seen from this angle, it appears that if by insurgency we mean only those militant armed activities aiming at political independence, the militant outfits, which can also be referred to as insurgent groups are not many. As on today only a few militant organizations like United Liberation Front of Assam (ULFA), National Socialist Council of Nagalim – Isak Muivah (NSCN-IM), National Socialist Council of Nagaland (NSCN-K), National Democratic Front of Bodoland (NDFB), People's Liberation Army (PLA), etc., can be termed as insurgent, in the sense that they have not yet given up openly their demand for sovereignty. But if one considers popular sympathy, support and participation also as criteria for calling their activities as insurgencies, it becomes difficult to say how many among them could be considered as insurgencies, since none of the militant organizations seem to exercise hegemony over the communities they claim to be working for. Yet one can broadly be referred to as insurgent groups, as they have been able to continue their militant activities against the Indian State for independence for several decades with the support of a section of the people belonging to the communities they claim to be representing.

Another issue which needs to be clarified is whether it is correct to use the expression, 'Insurgency in the Northeast'. For what we experience here in Northeast India is not insurgency (singular), but insurgencies (plural) of different kinds. Although certain factors such as geographical location, demographic composition, economic backwardness and colonial history of the region are common to all or to most insurgencies, particular factors that led the communities to insurgencies differ from one to another. Each insurgency in Northeast India is the result of a combination of a set of causes– general as well as particular. Our efforts to understand the roots of any insurgency in the Northeast should therefore concentrate on both general and particular factors.

Several militant groups in the region rationalize their demand for independence, by arguing that their communities had never been part of the empires and kingdoms that ruled the mainland India. The argument is defective because of two reasons: one, India did not exist as a political entity prior to the British occupation and second, there are several regions even in the mainland India, for example, South India, which almost remained independent of the rule of the emperors and kings that ruled the northern and central Indian subcontinent before the arrival of the British. It was only during the British rule that interior southern parts of India came under the control of external powers. Of course, it is true that the southern India had cultural, religious and economic linkages with northern India. But that is true of the many kingdoms (Koch, Kachari, Ahom, Meitei, and Tripuri) that ruled Northeast India as well. However, it needs to be admitted that before the British colonization quite a few hill tribes of the Northeast had very little or virtually no contact of any sorts – political, economic, religious or cultural - with the rest of the Indian subcontinent. Hence the pre-colonial history cannot be a proper explanation for insurgent movements in the region.

In my opinion, the major factor that made difference to Northeast India was the British rule. After the colonial occupation of the region, the British established direct rule only in the plains of Assam. In Manipur and Tripura the colonizers allowed the native kings to continue their rule, subject to their admission of the British paramountcy. The native rulers were prevented from exercising control of some of the peripheral regions inhabited by the hill tribes. Similarly, the hill areas of composite Assam inhabited by the indigenous tribes were treated as backward tracts and were declared as excluded or partially excluded areas. Those areas were all considerably left un-administered and were politically cut-off from the rest of India. This differential treatment of the regions and peoples of the Northeast during the British rule generated varied kinds of reactions in the region to the freedom struggle that took shape in the mainland India. The Indian nationalist movement did touch the plains of Assam, which were integrated with politics and economy of the rest of India. The educated middle classes and the peasants in the plains of Assam did identify themselves with India and participated actively in India's freedom struggle. In the partially excluded areas of composite Assam, such as Khasi-Jaintia Hills and Garo Hills, a few educated individuals who had the opportunity to study in cities such as Calcutta came in contact with Indian nationalist movement. But in the excluded areas of Assam and other un-administered hill areas of the Northeast, like the Naga Hills, the Lushai Hills, etc., the indigenous hill people virtually remained untouched by the Indian national movement. In the princely states of Manipur and Tripura, although the emerging educated middle classes were in touch with the political developments in the rest of India, they were more preoccupied with anti-feudal struggles against their own native rulers. Consequently pan-Indian identity among the masses in the princely states was not as strong as in the plains of Assam. In fact the anti-feudal struggles in the princely state of Manipur gave rise to Meitei nationalism. These differential attitudes of the communities and the regions in the Northeast to the Indian nationalist movement became the basis of different subsequent political developments and movements in the region, including insurgencies. Because of the unique colonial histories, the response of native communities in the region to the proposal for integration with the Indian Union ranged from one of active support to indifference to stiff opposition.

The next important factor that becomes relevant to the understanding of insurgencies in the region is the consequences of the birth of three sovereign states – India, Pakistan (now divided into Pakistan and Bangladesh) and Burma (Myanmar) in the region. Several areas inhabited by the indigenous nationalities and tribes in the region were divided among the newly formed nation-states. For no fault of their own, the native communities like Khasis, Garos, Kukis, Nagas etc., were separated and made the subjects of different nation-states. No efforts were made by the ruling elites of the newly formed nation-states to seek the consent of the native people. Naturally the native communities were resentful of the decisions taken by external powers and found it difficult to identify themselves easily with the nation-states that came to decide their fate. They suspected that their communities do not have a future in the newly formed states. It needed considerable political acumen on the part of the post-colonial elite in the newly formed nation-states to protect their political boundaries and strategic interests and at the same time to conceive of appropriate political arrangements that could douse the fears and suspicions of the native people and accommodate and satisfy the political aspirations of the native communities for self-rule. The failure of the ruling elites of the newly formed states in coming out with pragmatic strategies to deal with the existential dilemmas of the affected native communities, gave birth to ethnic identity movements, some of which later took the shape of insurgencies.

The Naga revolt against the Indian State, for example, is to be seen as the failure of the Indian political elite in creating confidence among the Nagas that their future as a community is safe and secure within the Indian Union. As they had little or virtually no contact with rest of the Indians, the Nagas found it difficult to identify themselves with the Indian State and the Indian people. Naturally, they had their doubts and fears about the consequences of joining the Indian Union. Instead of being sensitive to their suspicions and feelings, the Indian political elite then acted like a big brother and used its armed forces to integrate the Naga inhabited areas with the Indian Union as against the wishes of the Nagas. Therein lied the beginnings of Naga insurgency.

A section of the Mizos had same doubts and suspicions as the Nagas. But unlike the Naga leadership, the Mizos led by the Mizo Union showed its willingness to join the Indian Union, as the emerging educated Mizo elite then found in it an opportunity to get rid of the oppression and exploitation by the native tribal chiefs. After a decade and half the same Mizos felt let down by India when the Government of Assam failed to come to the rescue of the people in the Lushai Hills, when hit by the worst food crisis during the mid-sixties following the bamboo flowering. The dejected Mizos then extended their support to Lal Denga whose Mizo National Front (MNF) rose in revolt against the Indian State demanding independence. The insurgent leaders used the same language, arguments and rhetoric like the Nagas to justify their struggle for independence. Although the Mizo insurgency continued for more than a decade, it failed to win over the support of all Mizos. Realizing the limitations of the movement, in 1986 MNF leaders accepted a separate statehood within the Indian Union and joined the mainstream politics giving up their armed struggle.

In the valleys of Assam where both the masses and the leaders had actively participated in the anti-British movement led by the Indian National Congress, there was virtually no organized opposition from the Assamese people to Assam joining the Indian Union. It was only in the late seventies, after the All Assam Students Union (AASU) started the agitation against the Bangladeshi immigrants that a radical section within the Assam movement, who felt that India treated Assam only as a colonial hinterland and that Assam had no future within the Indian Union, formed ULFA in the year 1979 and declared war against the Indian State. The leaders of ULFA cited factors such as economic backwardness, underdevelopment, and decades of neglect of the region by the central government and the influx from Bangladesh and other states of India in justification of their fight against the Indian State.

In the erstwhile princely states of Manipur and Tripura, the native people and the native political leadership were considerably influenced by the developments in the mainland India. Powerful anti-feudal struggle that took place in the forties in both Manipur and Tripura were influenced to some extent by Indian National Congress (INC) and Communist Party of India (CPI). In Tripura although the pro-Indian sentiments were voiced mainly by the non-tribals, the tribal people did not show any organized opposition to Tripura joining the Indian Union. In fact the Maharaja of Tripura himself mooted the idea of Tripura joining the Indian Union. It was only when the waves of Bengali immigrants from the erstwhile East Pakistan, now Bangladesh, came and settled in Tripura in the subsequent decades making the tribal people the minorities in their own state, the tribal insurgency started gaining ground in Tripura. The experience in the princely state of Manipur was bit different. Although the native king did not command much of respect among the common people, the Machiavellian tactics that the Indian State adopted on the eve of independence to force the native king to integrate the state into the Indian Union had left deep scars in the minds of a section of the middle class Meiteis. But those hurt feelings did not give birth to insurgency at that point of time. The insurgency broke out only in the seventies, following the deep dissatisfaction among the educated middle class Meitei, who felt let down by both the state and the central governments that failed to bring about overall development of the state and its people. It was more to gain public support and sympathy for their insurgent activities that the Meitei militant groups chose to remind the people of the manner in which the Indian State forced the King of Manipur to merge the princely state of Manipur with the Indian Union in 1949.

The study shows that insurgencies took shape in different parts of the region, among different communities for different reasons. Although some militant groups have given up insurgency, one can still see insurgencies of different types and dimensions in different parts of the Northeast. In recent years the Indian State is indeed making efforts to negotiate with different insurgent groups and to bring them into the national mainstream. How far the peace efforts succeed depends on how effectively the Indian State understands the root causes of each of the insurgencies and finds pragmatic solutions to uproot them through appropriate political, economic and social interventions.

[For his presentation, Dr H Srikanth referred to the following works: H. Srikanth, "Insurgency and Counter-Insurgency: Agenda for Peace in India's North-east", in C. Joshua Thomas ed., *Polity and Economy: Agenda for Contemporary*

North East India, Regency Publications, New Delhi, 2005; Lt. Gen. N.S. Narahari, *Security Threats to North East India: The Socio-Ethnic Tensions*, Manas Publications, New Delhi, 2002; Sanjoy Hazarika, *Strangers of the Mist: Tales of War and Peace from India's Northeast*, Penguin, New Delhi, 1995; Sajal Nag, *Contesting Marginalities: Ethnicity, Insurgency and Subnationalism in North East India*, Manohar, New Delhi, 2002; All India People's Resistance Forum, *Symphony of Freedom: Papers on Nationality Question*, Hyderabad, 1996. - Editor].

3
PRESENTATION

—Rakhal Purkayastha

'Insurgency', in spite of being a term so widely used by administration and academia as well as man in the street, interestingly does not find entry in the *Encyclopaedia of Social Sciences* or *Britannica* or *Americana*. Most of the English dictionaries, including the *Oxford* and *Readers' Digest Great Illustrative Dictionary*, refer to it as an 'uprising' or an act of revolt against an established authority. V.K. Anand in his *Insurgency and Counter Insurgency: A Study of Modern Guerilla Warfare* considers insurgency as "an extra constitutional, competitively progressive and variegated struggle launched against the incumbent authority by a consciously mobilised section of indigenous masses for the fulfillment of certain conceptual goals manifesting emancipation" [1981, p. 28]. This definition emphasises the following characteristics of the insurgency: (a) it is an extra constitutional movement, (b) it is competitively progressive, (c) it is a movement against an established authority, (d) it is a mass based movement, and (e) it ultimately aims at emancipation. B. Pakem says that insurgency is "a reciprocal violence in which both the establishment and the challenger require the support and sympathy of a sizeable section of the society." [B. Pakem (ed), *Insurgency in North East India,* Omsons Publications, New Delhi, 1997, p. 9] S.K. Chaube correctly remarks on the problems associated with the definition of insurgency when he says that " to an established and legitimate authority, insurgency is a rebellion while to an insurgent it is an act of resistance or transformation." [S K Chaube, "Insurgency in Northeast India: A Heretical View" In B. Pakem (ed), *Insurgency in Northeast India,* Omsons Publications, New Delhi, 1997, p. 24] In fact, it is doubtful whether those whom we call as insurgents or as freedom fighters or defenders of their nation or as patriot etc do really accept the position of an established authority to be legitimate. Thus we feel this term 'insurgency' can be used only by those who are biased in favour of establishment.

North East India is an umbrella term which we frequently use to describe the states of Assam, Arunachal Pradesh, Mizoram, Manipur, Meghalaya, Nagaland and Tripura. The eighth state of Sikkim has been recently added for the purpose of development only. The region accounts for 8.06% of the total land surface of the country and has a population of 3.73% of the country's total. [*Annual Report 2004-05*, Ministry of Home Affairs, Govt of India, New Delhi, p. 32]. It is surrounded by China on the north, Myanmar on the east, Bangladesh on the south and Bhutan in the north-west. Nepal is not far away, and the only land connection with the mainland India is through a narrow corridor in the plains of North Bengal popularly known as 'chicken-neck'. It is through this narrow stretch flows the natural and finished resources and products such as tea, gas and crude out of the region, and consumers' goods, food and other essential and non-essential items into the region.

Topographically, 70% of the region is hilly and 88% of the population is rural based. Northeast is often described as 'Asia in miniature' where the brown and yellow races meet and mingle. This land of red rivers and blue mountains reportedly has as many as 350 communities and almost as many languages, many of the communities which have not been recognized are becoming increasingly vocal about their distinct culture and identity. Today, the people of the Northeast are uncertain of their present and equally apprehensive about what future holds for them. Rapid changes in social, political and economic spheres has taken place in the last fifty years or so in the region and the people are passing through what can be described as "one thousand years in a lifetime." [Lakshmi Krishnamurti, R Swaminathan, Gert W. Kueck (ed), *Responding to Terrorism*, Bookventure, Madras, 2003, pp. 94-103] Events are still moving at a terrific speed and people are overwhelmed at not being able to control the momentum or steer the movement in the direction they wanted. [Sanjoy Hazarika, "Ethnocentric Terrorism: Northeast: Building Bridges, Strengthening Civil Society", In *Responding to Terrorism: Dilemmas of Democratic & Developing Societies*, ed. Lakshmi Krishnamurti, R Swaminathan & Gert W Kueck, Bookventure, Madras, 2003, pp. 95-96].

India's northeast is considered one of the South Asia's hottest trouble spots with armed conflicts reported for the last fifty years or so. The Ministry of Home Affairs, Govt of India, reports for 2002-03 listed 24 active insurgent groups in the various states, besides many other inactive militant groups which continue to have the potential of flowering into an active group at any given moment. [*Annual Report 2002-03*, Ministry of Home Affairs, Govt of India, New Delhi] We feel that at least four general reasons have given rise to insurgency in the Northeast, viz. political isolation, economic underdevelopment and poorly developed infrastructure, immigration, and corruption among local politicians and elite.

The seeds of isolation and separateness of the Northeast from the rest of the country (British India) can be traced to the colonial past. Northeast was the last to come under the British rule. The region remained a part of the Lieutenant Governorship of Bengal till 1874. Its largest part became a Chief Commissionership, or a junior province, called 'Assam', on 6 February 1874. It was again amalgamated with East Bengal in 1905 (called 'Province of Eastern Bengal and Assam', under a Lt Governor, with Dhaka as headquarters) and separated in 1912. Assam became a Governor's province only in 1921. Manipur and Tripura remained princely states under British paramountcy. Arunachal area was administered as Frontier Tracts (first called North-East Frontier Tracts and later on – since 1943 - called NEFA, i.e. North-East Frontier Agency). The Inner Line Regulation was introduced in 1873 which drew an artificial line between the hills and the plains within the region. Under the Government of India Act 1919 the hill areas were declared to be backward tracts and under the Government of India Act 1935 the hills of the Northeast were categorized into Excluded and Partially Excluded Areas. Through these regulations the colonial rulers desired social, cultural, political and administrative segregation of the hills and plains. A section of the British administrators even toyed with the idea of a Crown's Colony consisting of the hills of Northeast India and Burma on the eve of India's independence but probably did not succeed as war ravaged Britain was not in a position to shoulder additional financial burden of a crown's colony and probably India's independence came earlier than it was expected.

It is widely accepted that continuing immigration from Bangladesh, actively encouraged by the politicians eager to fill their vote banks have brought about a rapid change in the demographic profile of the region. There has been also a continuous inflow of people from other regions of the country into the Northeast in search of employment and other avenues of livelihood. The region with limited scope of providing employment has further stretched the competition resulting into conflicts between insiders and outsiders, indigenous and aliens, locals and non-locals, etc. These conflicts have emerged as breeding grounds of insurgency. Educated unemployed, frustrated youths have become the new recruits of many of the insurgent groups.

The economic development in the region is characterized by trends as prevailing in the country as a whole. Despite efforts at policy formulation to cater to the needs of development of the north-eastern states, nothing significant has happened in last so many decades. The signs and symbols of development have not traveled beyond the capital towns or at best the urban centres. Much of the region still remains remote and inaccessible for most of the year. The region till now has remained what it was during the British colonial phase – the exporter of raw materials and importer of finished products. In spite of endless planning discourses and abundance of natural resources the industries have not come up especially in view of the lack of even basic infrastructure such as transport and communication and whatever has come have been mainly government units incurring losses after losses or small private industries to extract benefits of liberal subsidies and other tax benefits. Instead of contributing to the states, these industries have become a liability to the states and money earning gimmicks for the politicians and smart operators. The development in the Northeast has been caught up in the vicious cycle of industries not coming up due to insurgency and the insurgency thriving because of the lack of avenues for employment.

Finally, we cannot overlook the role of the local politicians in contributing to the cause of insurgency. The Government of India has not much of idea about the region and it feels that by pumping in money in the form of assistance, subsidy, special packages, relief, etc can solve the problems of insurgency along with military domination. Some of the local politicians have developed a vested interest in the violence to continue so that there is continuous inflow of funds to the states in the name of controlling the insurgency. The local politicians have displayed over the years that they have no political will to solve the problem of insurgency. Along with the contractors and bureaucrats, today the politicians have become the biggest beneficiary of all the money that comes from the Centre. There has been constant accusation of the politicians sponsoring, supporting and receiving kickback from certain insurgent groups. In such a situation the prospects of enduring peace in the region looks grim and bleak.

Before we end our discussion on insurgency it is important for us to consider the following points:

1. The region as a whole cannot be taken up for examining the roots of insurgency, as causes are generally area-specific

within the region. The Naga insurgency, for instance, originated in the 1950s due to geographical isolation and quest for distinct identity, the Mizo insurgency mostly revolved around economic conditions after the bamboo flowering, the Manipur insurgency can be traced to corruption and unemployment whereas the 1980s Assam insurgency along with Tripura insurgency can be traced to the large-scale influx of outsiders to the region.

2. Today what exists in the region in the name of insurgency no longer draws on romanticism and ideology that fired the imagination of the earlier groups in the past decades. Many of the groups of cadres, informers and leaders that exist do thrive on extortion and extraction from business houses, petty traders, contractors, government servants, politicians, etc. Insurgency has emerged as the fastest means to earn easy money. The number of fake groups and cadres far exceeds the real groups which points out as to how lucrative they have become. Most of the fake groups consists of petty criminals, school drop-outs, drug users, children from broken families, etc.

3. Much of the insurgency in the Northeast would not have remained without trans-border linkages. Earlier Pakistan and China used to be favourite destinations of the Northeast insurgents, later on it shifted to Bhutan, Myanmar and Bangladesh. The camps in Bhutan were destroyed in 2003 and today Bangladesh promises to be the favourite camping grounds for the groups where they are provided with facilities of terror strikes by the ISI of Pakistan. Though some of the camps continue to be in

Myanmar, the joint operations by forces of both the countries are not uncommon. [Wasbir Hussain, "Insurgency in India's Northeast, Cross-border Links and Strategic Alliances", www.google.com]

Our present discourse is limited to identifying the roots or causes of the insurgency (in fact, insurgencies) in Northeast India, as a methodological strategy to go step by step, but it goes without saying that the ultimate aim, like all other discourses on insurgency, is to find a solution to the problem, which it is possible only after the causes are known. Needless to say, it is much easier to point out the causes for insurgency rather than its solution. The region with 4500 kms of porous international borders will continue to simmer with low intensity conflicts in years to come unless we drastically improve our relations with our neighboring countries so that they do not become safe havens for the insurgent groups. But more importantly the solution has to come first from home; there is no alternative to a meaningful dialogue and addressing the larger issues that make the Northeast a 'boiling cauldron'. There has to be sincerity on the part of the government and a time frame before a dialogue is initiated, because if we look at the time taken by the Naga peace process then initiating and arriving at a solution with all the groups in the Northeast will probably take eternity. Along with dialogue much has to be done for the development of the region so that the fruits of development reaches the target groups for whom the development is intended, the central government must ensure efficient implementation of the various programmes and not resort to the rhetoric of Prime Minister's special packages which never reaches the people and at the same time ensure zero tolerance to all forms of corruption in the region.

4

PRESENTATION

—Surajit Sen

The First World War and the Second World War saw groups of nations collaborating against one another till the bombing at Hiroshima and Nagasaki clinched the bloodiest war in human history. But in the Third World War, we might never know who could be our enemy, but one could dare say that sixty years after the Second World, the Third World War is already being fought in country after country against an elusive enemy that has pooled into the punch a kind of invincibility arising from the element of surprise. And this enemy chooses its own time and place, using weapons that even the most powerful nation cannot even contemplate. It is the 'World' versus the 'Insurgents' operating from any part of the world that has kept every nation on tenterhooks. That the ranks of this enemy can recruit suicide squads for the bloody deeds makes them more powerful than the atom bombs. Their methodology could be different and the areas of operation might vary from time to time, but their ideology of hatred is too lethal to be counteracted by the war machinery or by the law and order enforcement agencies of various states. Blind with fury, they use the most vulnerable as the fodder for their common people – women, children and the unwary - anywhere in the world.

It is found that many people use 'terrorism' and 'insurgency' interchangeably, or at least, in the same sense. Actually, a distinction has to be made between the two. According to the *Oxford English Dictionary* (2005), terrorism is the use of violence and intimidation in an attempt to achieve political aims, while insurgency is a kind of rebellion or revolution. We may accept this distinction. Having thus distinguished insurgency from terrorism, it can be safely said that insurgency is an unsystematic use of terror in a variety of ways, by means of a sudden rebellion, to achieve some desired goals, by use of brute force.

Though insurgency cannot be confined to any single country or state or region, yet, speaking strictly in the Indian context, the main areas affected by insurgency are some southern states like Andhra Pradesh and Tamil Nadu, where LTTE has a big hold. In Central India and the North and the East, the states like Uttar Pradesh, Bihar, Jharkhand, Madhya Pradesh and West Bengal suffer from caste conflicts or sectarian violence which has often led to insurgent activities. But the worst affected states by insurgent activities are in the Northeast Region of the country. The states like Assam, Tripura and Manipur bear the major brunt of these activities. Meghalaya and Arunachal Pradesh are also affected by this malady. Mizoram suffered it for more than a decade. And Nagaland was the first state in the region to experience insurgency. The Naga insurgency, which started in 1950s, continues even today, although its form and methods have changed over the years.

The problem has sprouted over the years to engulf the entire region. Every year so many people are killed or kidnapped or extorted in the name of 'independence' or 'freedom'.

Geographically, the Northeast Region covers an area of 94,800 sq. kms with a population of over twenty-five million. It is comprised of seven states, viz. Arunachal Pradesh, Assam, Manipur, Meghalaya, Mizoram, Nagaland and Tripura. There is now one more, i.e. Sikkim, which has been made a member of the North-Eastern Council. The region is linked to the mainland India through a narrow 21 kms way, often called the 'chicken's neck', whereas India's international boundary in this region with Bangladesh, Myanmar, China and Bhutan runs to about 4,500 kms. It is also a land-locked area. Its boundary with so many countries has made the region politically very sensitive. Its strategic importance from the point of view of India's national security can hardly be overestimated.

The region has its own history. Be it the Ahom kings of Assam, or the kings of Tripura or Manipur, who lived in grand splendour, the history of the region goes back to Naraka and Bhagadatta of the epic age. The Mughals failed to occupy this region and the British conquest was not without stiff resistance which lasted almost for one hundred years. Each tribe has its own history that always has something to teach. Culturally, the region is diverse and unique. One is sure to find distinctions in language, dialects, clothes, food habits and many more. The societies in this region are pretty different from mainland India. This is mainly because of the presence of numerous tribes in the region. Christianity as a religion is practiced by more than two-third of the people living in the hill areas of the region. In the plains, Hinduism and Islam are dominant religions. There are some Buddhist tribes in Arunachal Pradesh and Upper Assam. There are also several indigenous religious practices. The caste-distinction is hardly a noticeable social phenomenon in the Northeast. Economically, this region is one of the most backward areas of India. There are hardly any major industries, except a few like the Digboi Oil Refinery, Mamlaw-Cherra Cement Factory and some paper and timber mills. Transport and communication system is still not satisfactory. There is mass unemployment and the population is growing almost like the rest of India. Basic infrastructure facilities like housing and health care are almost negligible in the remote areas of the region.

Once the geographical, historical, cultural, political and economic facts about Northeast India are studied, it may not be difficult to find out the roots or causes of insurgency in the region. It is not necessary to say that the geographical, historical and cultural features have made the Northeast a distinct or unique region in India; it is different from the rest of the country. Although there are physical and cultural diversities within the region and the different areas and tribes or communities have histories of their own, the economic and infrastructural backwardness that is so commonly imprinted all over the region has strengthened its regional identity. This has been possible by the policy of indifference and neglect of the Government of India towards the entire region.

Once we study the region, it is not difficult to find out the nature of insurgency in Northeast India and its causes. Though insurgency is not new to the region, there was hardly any serious attempt on the part of the government to control the problem. Several insurgent outfits, like NSCN (IM) in Nagaland, KYKL in Manipur, BLF in Mizoram, ULFA in Assam, and many others are still working through underground means. The lesser groups mainly resort to extortion, killings and kidnapping to make their presence felt in the region. Their main victims are the innocent and the helpless. Until the government takes appropriate steps to develop the region economically and remove the grievances of the people, the insurgency cannot be contained. To begin with, they should study the causes of insurgency.

The roots or causes of insurgency in Northeast India can be basically attributed to the social, economic and political scenario of the region. The causes can be broadly enumerated in the following way :

The Social Causes: 1.The problems of poverty and the exploitation of the vulnerable sections of the society can be said to be one of the main causes of insurgency in the Northeast. 2. Sometimes young persons become insurgents because they have a feeling of having been discriminated against and treated as second class citizens. 3. The appalling gap between the rich and the poor, the privileged and unprivileged also gives rise to rebellious tendencies. 4. Cultural clash, with the inter-mingling of various cultures, also gives rise to a feeling of loss of identity, which in turn results in attempts at saving the culture in the name of insurgency. 5. In many cases, it has been seen that brutal force is used by the high and mighty to settle personal scores. On the other hand, the social system is so partisan and corrupt that the victims of such highhandedness cannot secure any redress. It is such frustrated persons, who in utter desperation ultimately take up guns.

The Economic Causes: 1. Northeast is essentially economically backward in terms of infrastructure and industrialization. This means the limitation of employment opportunities. As a natural corollary, the youths are swayed to commit unpardonable acts of rebellion, for they think that the best way to give vent to their indignation and frustration is to take up guns. 2. It can be contended that the youths in this vulnerable area do not have simple opportunities for their overall development. Hence, to give meaning to their aspirations they have resorted to underground movements. 3. The growing inequality in the society due to uneven development and the monopolization of all privileges and facilities by a small group of neo rich is another important cause of social tension which provokes the marginalized and the exploited to revolt against the existing social order.

The Political Causes: 1. It has often been noticed that power turns the heads of the political upstarts, and they go to any extent to use their power. When the life of the victims of blatant abuse of power becomes meaningless and they find no difference between life and death, they resort to insurgent activities in the false hope that in this way they can attain a glorious end. 2. The concept of 'sons of soil' is likely to have led to some sort of a regional arrogance, which might have culminated in the form of insurgent activities in the region. 3. Patronage from some political parties and leaders has also led to insurgent acts in the region.

In conclusion it may be said that 'Insurgency' is undoubtedly the ugliest face of dissent. This phenomenon should be condemned universally and unequivocally. However, unless corrective measures are evolved by the government to wean away the path of violence by providing the youths with enough educational facilities and employment avenues, and the feeling of discrimination and deprivation is removed by accelerating economic growth, there is always the danger of spurt in insurgent activities in the Northeast and in the whole country.

5

PRESENTATION

—Jayati Bhattacharjee

I agree with the views expressed by the senior scholars that there are several roots or causes of insurgencies in Northeast India, that there are various models or formats of insurgency in the region, that the insurgency has been going on in the region for a long time, and that there are different causes for the different forms of insurgency at different points of time and in various parts of the region. However, I look upon the contemporary state of insurgency as primarily a problem of the youths, because the insurgents or militants mostly include young generation of the population – educated or drop-outs from high schools and colleges. Though some of them are elders by now, these elders had also formed or joined the groups when they were young. This makes the phenomenon of insurgency more disturbing for the simple reason that the youths can never be destructive by nature. They are embodiments of hope and energy, on which depends the future of a society and a nation. It is said that youth is the age of dream - the dream of a bright future, and it is this dream of a future that propels the youths to constructive and meaningful actions. It may be true that they are sometimes angry, and argumentative, and do protest against what they consider wrong or unfair. But the protest does not mean violence. The protests of the youths generally mean democratic movements, which have occurred in the twentieth century in various countries, including India, and which are continuing all over the world even today with the acceptance of democracy as the most popular political order. The instances of violence in such movements are very few, and the exceptions are considered as mere aberrations. On the contrary, the Northeast today represents a scenario of 'youth and violence'. Therefore, the basic question is : Why are the young people of the region so angry that they opted for the dangerous path of armed struggles or insurgency ?

The answer to this question is embodied in the series of complaints and demands made by the students' and youths' organizations (and even others) on the infrastructural and economic development of the region in 1960s and 70s. By then the unemployment problem had already become insurmountable, and the educated unemployed youths were everyday becoming more and more restless. But those democratic complaints and demands fell into deep ears. The Government of India took no initiative to respond to the genuine problems and legitimate aspirations of the youths of the region. The anger of the youths gradually reached the breaking point. And the contemporary state of insurgencies in the region started in the later part of 1970s. I am not talking of the insurgencies in Nagaland, Manipur and Mizoram, which occurred much earlier and were considered as isolated or sporadic events. But the insurgencies which commenced in late-1970s moved very fast to cover almost the entire region within a decade. Therefore, I consider the current state of insurgency and militancy as a reaction of the youths of the region to the indifferent attitude of the central government and its regional agencies towards the problems of the Northeast.

As a matter of fact, the indifferent attitude of the Government of India towards the north-eastern region since independence has resulted in the economic backwardness and under-development of this part of the country. The government showed no interest in industrialization and infrastructure development, despite abundant forest and mineral resources of the region. As a result, the job opportunities could not be created sufficiently. Only the central and state government offices could employ educated youths in administrative and clerical posts. Another sector was the teaching profession - in schools and colleges. But these sources also became dry within few years after independence. On the other hand, the population in the region was growing at much higher rate than the national average, and so also the number of the educated unemployed youths. The state governments could not create unlimited number of posts due to their own constraints, and in course of time, some of them introduced a ban on filling up the vacancies and in some cases, even resorted to abolition of posts. The problem of unemployment was compounded by the fact that the number of schools, colleges, and universities went on increasing. They continued to produce thousands of educated youths every year. By 1960s, the educated unemployment problem had already become a serious one and the educated young people suffered disappointment and frustration. The government did not take a serious note of the situation. There was nothing like manpower planning, nor any initiative to create job opportunities. The natural resources remained mostly unexplored and unutilized. Only a portion of the raw-materials used to be taken out for processing in factories outside the region. Naturally, this did not yield any benefit to the region. The policy of indifference and neglect on the part of the central government thus caused inadequate avenues of employment for the educated youths as well as improper garnishing of the resources of the region. The frustrated youths were, therefore, compelled to search for an effective method to express their grievances.

If we delve into the history of the region since independence we will find that the Northeast was indeed already a backward region in 1947 as compared to other regions of the country. Over and above, to its plight was added a number of factors caused by the partition of the country – (i) the region lost its shorter and direct route to Calcutta and rest of India through East Bengal, (ii) the traditional border trade became almost extinct, and above all, (iii) the uprooted religious minorities from East Pakistan migrated to this region in large number. The government took no noticeable step to rebuild the shattered economy of the region or to accelerate the process of development. There was no industry worth the name. Tea industry was getting exhausted, and agriculture suffered stagnation and deterioration. On the other hand, the natural resources or the raw-materials were taken outside the region for processing and the manufactured goods from other regions were marketed here. It reflected a dichotomous situation which was not much different from the India-Britain economic relationship during the early colonial period. The wholesale business was in the hands of the outsiders, particularly the Marwaris, Sindhis, Gujaratis and the Punjabis. The youth from this region hardly looked for employment anywhere outside the region, whereas a large number from other regions were provided employment here - both in public and private sectors. This situation was responsible for the growth of ill-feeling against the outsiders, the cry for 'son of the soil', and social tensions.

Many in the position of authority are these days heard to blame the insurgency as being responsible for not allowing the development to take place in the region. They often forget that although during the first 20 years after Independence there was no insurgency as such, no initiative was noticed on the part of the central government for the development of the region. In that period the Naga insurgency was the only insurgency that mostly affected only the Naga areas in Nagaland and Manipur. The rest of the region was in peaceful conditions. The cry for 'son of the soil' or 'local-outsiders' problem also had not surfaced so prominently as in subsequent years. If the government had the will to develop the road and railway network and to industrialize the region in that period there would be no difficulty or opposition for them. Moreover, for the marginal development that took place, like extension of the railways and conversion of the meter gauge into broad gauge, establishment of oil refineries or paper mills or even universities, technical institutions and medical colleges, the students and youths of the region had to agitate for a long time, suffer the gallows of the administration, and some even became martyrs. In the mean time, the number of educated youths increased manifold. But they were without avenues of employment. This army of unemployed educated youths became very large over the years, and they suffered frustration and disappointment. They compared the region with other parts of the country which were progressing steadily. Their anger fell on the central government for the discrimination. All these might be responsible for provoking the young men and women of the region to take to militancy and insurgency to draw the attention of the national authority to the problems of the region and to compel the latter to find some solutions for the unemployment problem and infrastructural backwardness of the region. The militancy also provided a section of the youths with employment and money. Some of them are said to have formed groups only for extortions and ransoms. The unemployment problem is thus so closely related to insurgency and militancy of various types. Had the region been adequately developed economically and infrastructurally by exploring and utilizing the natural resources and surplus manpower of the region itself the educated unemployment problem would not be so alarming, and the insurgency and militancy would not have taken such ugly turns.

In recent years, the Government of India seems to be keen on the development of the Northeast. Its programmes and policies include the signing of accords promising infrastructural growth, development packages, non-lapsable pool, directive to all central ministries to spent at least 10% of the funds on the Northeast, and finally, a separate ministry for the Development of the North-Eastern Region (DONER).We also hear about the 'look east' policy and the Asian Highway. But all these initiatives are only after so many years of insurgency and militancy. While appreciating these initiatives and generosity, it must be said that there are many who consider these efforts as weaknesses of the central government and as success of the militancy. This has also come indirectly as an encouragement to the militancy, because many think that while the government may not normally approve some development projects for certain areas the militants' threat may do the job. In the name of rehabilitation of the surrendered militants, the state governments are already getting additional financial support. The fingers are also raised on the quality of execution of works and the honesty and accountability of the officials responsible for the implementation of the projects. Nevertheless, it is good that the government has taken note of the economic backwardness of the region and, though belatedly, the people may hope that the development will now take place through the DONER and the revamped NEC (North Eastern Council).

It goes without saying that the recent initiative for economic development of the region is an acceptance by the Government of India of the fact that they neglected the development of the Northeast for a long time and that the economic backwardness and the lack of opportunities are reasons behind the current phase of insurgency in the region. In fact, when the All Assam Students Union (AASU) launched the movement for the detection and deportation of the foreign nationals the radical section within the Assam Movement campaigned that the central government had been treating Assam as an economic hinterland and an internal colony of India. This section eventually formed the United Liberation Front of Assam (ULFA) and cited the economic backwardness, underdevelopment, and neglect of Assam since the independence of India, and the influx from Bangladesh, Nepal and also other regions of India, as justifications of their demand for the liberation of Assam. The turmoil spread very fast to other parts of the region, where similar groups and demands began to surface, for the simple region that those areas were also economically backward and the same sentiments were working in those areas also. In Tripura the influx from Bangladesh had taken place since the partition of India (1947), but 1979 saw the outbreak of violence against the Bengalis. This was followed by the emergence of insurgent outfits for the liberation of the indigenous ethnic groups in Tripura. As a matter of fact, the cry for the 'son of the soil', which was going on in many parts of the region, originated in the fact that the opportunities were so limited and the limited number of jobs and other opportunities had to be shared by the local youths with others. Had those opportunities been created sufficiently the hatred for new-comers and outsiders would not be there. But such opportunities were not abundantly available because of the economic and infrastructural backwardness of the region. It may not be wrong to say that the demand for jobs for the local people matured into insurgency and militancy. These facts prove it beyond doubt that the current phase of insurgency which began with the Assam Movement and the formation of ULFA (1979) are rooted in the economic backwardness of Northeast India. Even in cases of the earlier insurgencies the economic factor cannot be overlooked. It is true that the insurgencies in Nagaland and Manipur originated in the complaints that those areas were retained or integrated in India, after the end of the British rule, without the consent of the people. But over the years, the government should have been able to convince the people by accelerating the economic development that they are sure to gain as being in India. The educated youths, who had been swelling the ranks of the insurgent cadres, could be dissuaded provided they were assured of suitable jobs and decent living. The Mizos had no movement against the Indian state during or after the transfer of power. Though a small section had initially some reservations about remaining in India after independence, they were ultimately convinced by the Mizo Union and the dusts settled down within few years. But the outbreak of insurgency in 1966 was directly on economic ground. There were instances of bamboo flowering notifying sufficiently the possibility of the outbreak of famine conditions. The elders cautioned the administration, but the Government of Assam (of which the Mizo Hills was then a district) did nothing to avoid the impending famine. When the famine actually broke out, there was acute shortage of food stuff. The only one road that connected Mizo Hills with the rest of India, namely, the Silchar-Dwarband-Aizawl Road, was for the most part bridle and not workable in the monsoons. The insurgents destroyed one or two wooden bridges and that was enough for snapping connections with India. The Mizo National Front (MNF), under the leadership of Lal Denga, formed its own underground administration. The army came in picture and the rice bags were air dropped, but those hardly reached the people. The belated efforts to give relief to the famine stricken people were not enough to persuade the insurgents to give up arms. The failure of the Government of Assam to prevent the famine is seen as the immediate cause for the outbreak of insurgency in Mizo Hills. However, the overall economic and infrastructural backwardness are the ultimate facts behind the insurgency. This is further proved by the fact that the creation of the Union Territory of Mizoram, and later on its elevation to statehood, changed the situation. A new Silchar-Aizawl Road (via Vairengti) was constructed as an all-weather road and development projects were taken up by the state government. Mr Lal Denga and his followers ultimately shunted the path of violence and returned to the mainstream politics. In fact, Lal Denga's party (MNF) participated in elections to the Mizoram Assembly and the Indian Parliament. Lal Denga himself became the Chief Minister of Mizoram for a term before his death. Today, Mizoram is said to be one of the most peaceful states in India.

Finally, that the economic backwardness was a very important cause of the insurgency has been accepted by the Prime Minister, Dr Manmohan Singh. Addressing the Chief Ministers' Conference in 2005, he said: "Inadequate employment opportunities, lack of access to resources, underdeveloped agriculture, artificially depressed wages, geographical isolation, lack of effective land reforms may all impinge significantly on the growth of extremism." I agree with the Prime Minister, and I do strongly believe that the economic backwardness, which is also responsible for causing unemployment and lack of opportunities, is the root cause of insurgency in Northeast India.

6
PRESENTATION

—Vareipam Muivah

Insurgency has by now become a part of life in Northeast India. We hear about so many insurgent and militant groups and their so many demands. There is no single cause or factor responsible for the emergence and sustenance of insurgencies in this part of the country. It is indeed a combination of several conditions that constituted the roots of insurgencies. Among the more important causes are the isolation of the region from the rest of India, distinctive history and culture of the peoples of the region, lack of integration of the region culturally, socially and economically with the rest of India, very poor road network and other means of communication, economic backwardness leading to rampant unemployment and widespread poverty, lack of appropriate educational facilities, maladministration, corruption, and, above all, faulty policies of the erstwhile British Government and of the Government of India in respect of the Northeast. However, the existence of some ethnic sub-national groups wanting to secede from India constituted the most significant root of insurgencies in the Northeast.

It is important to note that there are some genuine insurgent groups in Northeast India who enjoyed the mass support of their respective ethnic societies and they had the conscious demand and clear vision of liberating their ethnic areas which were forcibly occupied by the British and handed over to the Indian state without taking peoples' sentiments into account. They believe that they have distinctive identities defined by their history and socio-economic and cultural life. They look upon themselves as unique ethnic groups, different from the rest of the communities in India, and different even from their immediate neighbours, and they consider their claim to secede from the Indian Union as genuine. This does not, however, mean that the insurgencies in some cases have not degenerated from its original position. There are instances of rampant indiscipline and corruption among them, and they use the platform for self-interests and self-promotion among some sections of the leadership and the rank and file of the insurgents. Such degeneration is due to human weaknesses for wealth and power about which we have so many instances in history of the mankind. The insurgency or any sustained struggle against a powerful authority always requires strong character on the part of the leaders and cadres of the struggle. They must be committed and dedicated souls, who are incorruptible and without greed and temptation. On the other hand, there are individuals, even in the rank and file of the insurgents, who could not resist the hunger for wealth and power, and they became easy prey in the hands of those who wanted to destroy the cause of the insurgents by demoralizing them. The factionalism, loss of character, and the emergence of multiple outfits from the ranks of the same cause are the results of human weaknesses on the part of the insurgents themselves.

Nonetheless, there are some insurgent groups and leadership who have genuinely continued to struggle and suffer for the sake of the original goal of liberation.

Having said this, we also have to take cognizance of the fact that there are many groups which operate in the name of insurgents in the Northeast though they do not fit into the category of insurgents technically and definitionally. They are only after their own selfish interests, which they aim at achieving by using militant means. They have no ideology or social commitment. The people will never support them once their true character is known. These groups should be dealt with strongly by the authorities (both central and state) as a matter of general law and order problem. They should be isolated from the masses by exposing their true colour. Normalcy and peace, as far as these groups are concerned, can be brought through active policing, inducing strong motivation in the youth and providing quality education in a planned manner over a period of time. On the other hand, the problem of the genuine insurgents operating in the region should be addressed by the concerned authorities with an open and sincere mind and they should work for a politically negotiated settlement which should be acceptable to all the concerned parties so that perpetual peace and develop-ment may reign in the region.

In my opinion, the failure of the government to distinguish between the genuine and the pseudo insurgents is responsible for the continuation of the state of insurgency for such a long period. The government also failed to see the political significance of the insurgency when it first broke out in the

Naga hills and wanted to handle it as a mere law and order problem. Thereby, they complicated the matter. May be, Delhi was not properly informed by the local administration that the Naga National Council enjoyed the mass support of the Naga people for a political settlement of the Naga problem. On the other hand, the insurgency was a war against the Indian State for liberation of the Naga people. The Naga leaders made their intentions clear much before the independence of India. Neither had they participated in the framing of the Indian Constitution nor did they accept it. They declared the Nagas as a separate nationality, established international contacts, and looked upon their struggle as a national war. The Indian leadership of the time did not take them seriously. At the same time, the administrative and police excesses and the cruel torture by the army and the police, while trying to suppress the insurgency as a law and order problem, made the Naga people more determined to achieve their cause. The administration also sometimes adopted the underhand methods of effecting splits in the insurgents' ranks to make them fight each other. There were innumerable fratricidal murders and killings. The administration also created its own followers who were projected as leaders and the government negotiated with them. The Government of India unilaterally converted the Naga Hills district of Assam into the state of Nagaland. It did not satisfy the insurgents. Later on, of course, the government realized the need for political settlement with the leaders of insurgency and there were some rounds of talks and dialogues. But these also did not bring peace, mainly because of three reasons; firstly, it was too late, secondly, some of the talks were not with the genuine leadership of the insurgency, and thirdly, when it was with the real leaders the latter suspected the sincerity of the government to resolve the issues, and as a result, the talks ended in failures. In the meantime, insurgency spread to other parts of the Northeast when more and more ethnic groups demanded secession or autonomous state or sub-state, or regional autonomous council by adopting violent means. Some of these are technically not insurgencies. The confusion was confounded further when groups of unemployed youths formed armed groups for the purpose of financial extortions and personal gains. The administration confused them with the insurgents. Therefore, my conclusion is that the wrong policies and inefficiencies of the government and the local administration, their lack of knowledge of history and culture of the people of this region, and the indifference and apathy of the Indian leadership towards the region, are the roots of insurgencies in Northeast India.

7
PRESENTATION

—Joydeep Bhattacharjee

I would like to share my personal views on insurgency that I experienced as a journalist while working in states like Meghalaya, Assam, Arunachal Pradesh, Mizoram and Sikkim for various newspapers (regional and national) and a portion of my study on social structure and social movements in Northeast India vis-à-vis movements for self-assertion.

Insurgency or terrorism, violence or social conflicts, the north-eastern states are suffering from such turmoil for over five decades and as far as my study goes, the root cause lies in isolation of people of the region because of the isolationist policies adopted by the Government of India from time to time having their origination in India under the British imperialism. I am in agreement with Professor J B Bhattacharjee who rightly pointed out that the British imperialists had separate policies for different areas, which segregated the hill tribes in the region. To my understanding, differential policies during the British colonial era caused more harm than doing any benefit to many of the tribes, which are now torn between development and modernism. One can refer to the introduction of Inner Line Permit, commonly known as ILP, by the British for some parts (now states) of the Northeast. It was brought into effect on the pretext of 'safeguarding the hill tribes' from the influential cultural groups from the plains.

Independent India, which still has colonial hangover, no doubt had more influence of their leaders during initial days of post-Independence. This saw the framing of the Indian Constitution as an exercise of replicating what some other countries already had, without considering the ground realities in India. This in many cases proved to be hasty and thoughtless. I remember attending an workshop at the North-Eastern Hill University, Shillong, on constitutional review, which was, among others, addressed by Dr Subhash C Kashyap, former secretary-general of the Lower House of Indian Parliament and Constitutional Adviser to the Indian Government, who during his deliberation on the flaws in Indian Constitution, referred to the Father of the Constitution Dr B R Ambedkar as saying: "If I find the constitution being misused, I shall be the first to burn it." In this context, one can construe that Dr Ambedkar knew that the Constitution that he scripted would be misused for it has some inherent discrepancies.

Here I would like to focus on ILP, which was allowed to continue even after so many years of country's Independence.To my belief and understanding, ILP was framed to keep the hill tribes in the Northeast, besides other parts of British India, aloof and away from the light of development. It is almost like keeping a specimen in a zoo for the developed animal like man to come and visit them once in a while, be it for academic reasons or just for leisure. Not realising the cascading effects of allowing such a system to continue, we continued to keep this group of people in the region isolated for years together. This can be termed as 'protective isolation', which in the name of safeguarding some communities, kept them isolated, disallowing their legitimate rights to develop and grow together with the whole nation and the humankind. Ironically, these human groups or peoples took ILP as a system, which they believed, would keep outsiders (people from mainland India) away and would prevent them from inundating the tribal land. They also preferred the continuance (as for Nagaland, Mizoram and Arunachal Pradesh) or introduction (as in Meghalaya and some other parts of the Northeast) of ILP. This has actually convinced the peoples (different groups of people having different cultural identities) in the Northeast to believe that they are different from other peoples coming from mainland India and resulted in a peculiar psyche to rebel against the whole lot, which actually came to govern their activities in later stage. Actually, these discriminatory policies and systems resulted in psychological distances becoming more deep-rooted than the physical distance from the national capital. More importantly, these policies not only segregated the tribes in the Northeast from the rest of the country but also distanced one group from another within the region.

Similarly, the reservation policy also segregated people instead of uniting them or helping the weak or deprived lot to actually grow and improve. In the Northeast, we see that such policies helped only a section of the people who are fortunate to reap the benefits, while others remained backward or poor and deprived even today. This policy has divided the traditionally egalitarian tribal societies into forward and backward, rich and poor. The common people even do not understand who are actually responsible for their backwardness and poverty, because the forward section do point fingers towards Delhi and the outsiders only.

I feel that today's insurgency is a manifestation of the growing frustrations among the deprived lot of people in each tribe or community, who saw a small section within their community improving and growing. This resulted in a growing gap between the 'haves' and 'have-nots' within one community, and naturally, the disgruntled lot saw evils in Indian policy and system of governance and stood up to challenge the country's seat of power. If we look carefully, we can see that the 'have-nots' chose to fight the foreign elements (here people from other cultural and linguistic backgrounds) than fighting their own people. In Meghalaya, most of the militant cadres come from the under-developed areas. It is a known fact that most of the HNLC cadres are from Mawlai, a relatively backward area in Shillong and from West Khasi Hills, the most backward district in the state. It was expected that the respective individual community would ponder over this and would bring some changes in their attitude towards their own people, instead of instigating the disgruntled ones to turn the guns towards others. The enlightened people from individual communities are expected to understand themselves and also to make others understand that such violent movements in the name of secession do not harm others but ownselves only. Then only a united voice can be raised to protest against the discriminatory policies of the government, instead of fighting the mighty force involved in the protection of country's integrity. Unfortunately, no such initiative was noticed in the region when it was needed.

I also feel that the organization or reorganization of states has not been congenial to India's nation building processes. The creation of various states on the basis of majority people's language further divided the people and gave rise to identity crisis for many smaller linguistic groups. For instance, in Assam the hill state movement in 1960s was a direct consequence of the policy of the state government to make Assamese the only official language of the state. The government and the state assembly on that occasion acted under pressure from the Assamese people who constituted the majority population in the state. Later on, we saw the rise of the Bodo movement against the Assamese domination on the ground of identity crisis. Initially they wanted a separate state for them, but then settled with an autonomous council. However, the National Democratic Front of Bodoland (NDFB) is still for a separate state. The Bodo insurgency (in fact, militancy) is actually for a separate state within India; they never asked for a sovereign state. The Autonomous State Demand Committee (ASDC) has been demanding an autonomous state within Assam consisting of the Karbi Anglong and the North Cachar Hills districts. Incidentally, these are the only two remaining hill districts in Assam which were given the option either to join Meghalaya or to remain in Assam when Meghalaya was created as an autonomous state in 1970 consisting of the Khasi-Jaintia and the Garo hills districts. Within few years, however, the people, particularly the youths, in Karbi Anglong and North Cachar, became disillusioned with Assam complaining that the state government was discriminating in matters of economic development and that there was a crisis of identity. The ASDC launched a peaceful democratic movement. The party won majority of seats in Autonomous District Council in both the districts, majority of the seats in these two districts to the Assam Legislative Assembly and the lone seat to Lok Sabha in last two decades. They asked for an autonomous state within Assam, and never talked of separation from India. However, the delay of the government in conceding the demand angered a section of the Karbi youths who resorted to militancy. That is how we hear of the 'Karbi militants'. But this militancy is not against the Indian state, and therefore, cannot be termed as insurgency. Nevertheless, the ASDC is still pursuing its demand for an autonomous state. A strong section of the Dimasa youths were not interested in going with the Karbis in a common state in which the Karbis would be in the majority. They also wanted that the Dimasa areas in the Karbi Anglong and the Cachar districts of Assam and the Dimasa areas in Nagaland, besides the North Cachar Hills district of Assam, should be in one Dimasa state. They did not like the idea of a sub-state within Assam, but wanted a full-fledged Dimasa state within India to be called 'Dimaraji'. Therefore, the Dima Halam Daoga (DHD) is demanding a separate state for the Dimasas to be carved out of the Dimasa inhabited areas of Assam and Nagaland. They did not go for the democratic processes of participating in elections, etc, but resorted to militant means. Nevertheless, they are not asking for secession from India. An almost similar situation we witness in case of the Naga movement, where the insurgents now are demanding Greater Nagaland with integration all Naga populated areas within India, viz. some adjoining portions of Assam, Ukhrul and Senapati districts in Manipur, Tirap and Changlang districts in Arunachal Pradesh, and their unification under the new concept. Major repercussions of this latest demand of the Naga insurgents have been seen in Manipur. On the other hand, in Manipur, we have as many as 30 insurgent groups active. This is just an indication of to what direction such movements in Northeast may lead us to. Meghalaya also acts as an example, where 30 years after the formation of the hill state, we are now again faced with separatist movements, though political in nature, favouring further division of the state, viz., the Khasi-Jaintia State and the Garoland.

The examples, cited above, are enough to prove that all the militant or terrorist groups in Northeast India are not necessarily insurgents. They are not fighting for secession or separation from India, but for autonomy for their respective ethnic or linguistic areas. These demands do come in because the ethnic and linguistic minorities have a feeling that the dominant ethnic or linguistic groups in the state, who are in majority in the government, are discriminating against the minority areas in matters of development and that the cultural identity of the minorities is in danger. As smaller groups, they do not expect to get justice through democratic movements, since such movements are easily crushed by the dominant section by use of the political power of the state machinery. This issue also brings out the question of the minority (ethnic and linguistic) policy of the central government in the Indian states. The problem started with the concept of the linguistic states, although the states included areas in which the ethnic and linguistic minorities are indigenous and in absolute majority in their own areas. The ethnic or linguistic majority for the purpose of the reorganization of states in 1954 meant only a simple majority in the total population of the whole state. In case of Assam, the Assamese had a thin majority, and that too, how this was achieved by tempering with the 1951census is a known fact in history. Assam included such districts, and tribal blocs and belts, in which the respective ethnic and linguistic groups (though minority in the state) were absolute and those areas never formed parts of Assam before the British rule and had no indigenous Assamese population. Yet, the central government did nothing to protect the cultural identities of the minorities when the state government pursued a policy of 'assimilation' or 'Assamese-ization'. In my opinion, the concept of linguistic state and linguistic minority policy of the central government should be seen as important roots of the unrest (or 'insurgency') in Northeast India.

While we are blaming the foreign countries for aiding and abetting insurgency in Northeast India, we need to understand that a country like Bangladesh benefit a lot from these insurgents as they take shelter on its soil. By helping various insurgent groups from Northeast India in developing their armoury, Bangladesh benefits extremely by selling arms and weapons, besides imposing huge tax on every consignment reaching on its ports, like Cox's Bazar, from other countries sympathetic to these groups. Also most of the insurgent leaders from Northeast India are settled in countries like Bangladesh and Thailand and they are investing the extorted money in those countries. For instance, intelligence reports have it that Paresh Baruah and many senior leader of ULFA have invested crores of rupees in the hotel sector and many of these international standard hotels are running in Dhaka and paying huge tax to the Bangladesh Government. As a result, we never hear any voice of concern being raised by these insurgent groups against the infiltrators or illegal settlers from Bangladesh. The Government of India's failure to diplomatically deal with those foreign countries, which are directly or indirectly promoting insurgency in Northeast India, is another important root of insurgency in the region.

Finally, as someone has pointed out, we must address the question whether we should continue to use the terms like 'insurgency', 'insurgencies' or' social movements' to define the violent movements that are going on in the Northeast. I believe that these movements can't be termed as insurgency, insurgencies or for that matter, social movements. Most of these movements are political in nature and they constitute a part of regional political movements in the Northeast against the national parties, which they believe have their own set of ideas that are not relevant to the Northeast. In my opinion, the movements in Northeast India are not far in nature from those of groups like the Ranbir Sena, which is, at least to me, an armed wing to ensure supremacy of the higher caste politicians, and the Naxalites, for the deprived lot, who are fighting their violent political battles for so many years. Some of the groups in the Northeast also come very close to those in other parts of India where we see bloody skirmishes between various groups for having political control over people and the state. Most of the insurgent groups in the Northeast are also fighting for the causes which were outlined by the ethno-regional political parties. The political control over the state and the people happen to be the ultimate motivation of the insurgency in the Northeast also. If we look into the history of insurgency in the Northeast, we find that the Naga insurgency began with a demand for having absolute political control over land and people. They wanted to be 'self ruled', which means total control over governance, policy making and enactment of rules and regulations. They started believing that such an atmosphere could be created only through absolute freedom and secession from India. For Assam, it is in history that former Chief Minister Prafulla Kumar Mahanta, when he was President of the All Assam Students Union (AASU), had a secret meeting, during the course of the Assam Movement, with Paresh Barua and Arabindo Rajkhowa, two radical activists of the movement, and it was decided in that meeting to have one armed wing and another political wing of the movement to fight for their legitimate rights. That is how the United Liberation Front of Assam (ULFA) came into being and the Assam Gana Parishad (AGP) was formed. Nevertheless, the members from both the wings eventually lost their original objectives and gradually drifted from each other, which in the later stage, snowballed into extreme enmity between the two groups. The historical backgrounds are similar for the formation of Hynniewtrep National Liberation Council (HNLC) and the Achik National Volunteers Council (ANVC) in Meghalaya. The ANVC found that the Garo Hills did not benefit much from the state which was mainly governed by the Khasi Ministers, and so they voiced the demand for a separate state, while the HNLC came into existence following non-implementation of the Instrument of Accession, which had assured them of having rights over land, water, forests and minerals. It is said that when for almost fifty years the Instrument of Accession did not materialise, some of the radicals in Meghalaya, who came in touch with Naga insurgents in the Shillong Jail, finalised their decision to form Hynniewtrep Achik Liberation Council

(HALC). Later on, Achik and Hynniewtrep broke apart and we find the formation of today's HNLC and ANVC. Given this situation, would I be very wrong in saying that the movements in the Northeast are more political in nature? As I strongly believe that India must rectify the flaws in nation building process and discrimination in the policy making, I also feel that each community must raise this issue within their own community to adopt the right path to voice their protest, be it against anything. In any democracy, dissent should be decent enough to suit the civilised culture. The roots of insurgency lie in what we lack or where our system fails.

8
PRESENTATION

—L S Gassah

It may be possible to identify or find out the 'roots' of insurgency in Northeast India, but these 'roots' may not be the same in all the situations as far as the North-Eastern States of India are concerned. What was or is applicable in one or two states of the region may not be the same for all the states. For example, the 'roots' of insurgency in Nagaland or Mizoram may not be the same as in Assam or Meghalaya or Manipur. Sometimes, some scholars tend to point out that these are the roots of insurgency in the states of Northeast India, whereas in reality, they are not 'roots' but 'influence' only of one insurgent group on others. Thus, these two things – 'roots' and 'influence' are to be separately identified and analysed. The two are not to be used interchangeably as they represent two different aspects of the same issue. Further, in one particular state, it might be the roots of insurgency but on the other state, it may turn out to be the 'influence' of a group of insurgents on the other. The two issues may also be separated on the basis of the time that insurgency got started in a particular area or state of the region and how that same idea influenced the others at a later stage. It is therefore very important to differentiate between 'roots' and 'influence' of one insurgent group on the other or others. On the other hand, those insurgent groups who have been 'influenced' by the activities or actions of others must have considered the matter or things that happened around them seriously before launching the insurgent programmes or following the footsteps of others. As far as the factors or reasons for being influenced as such are concerned, it is very difficult to point out specifically at this stage. Such factors may not also be universally applicable to all. They are surely different from time to time and from one state to another or more specifically, from one ethnic area to another within the same state.

In our effort to find out 'roots' of insurgency in Northeast India, it may be necessary to trace certain historical developments relating to society, culture, tradition and custom, language/dialect, routes of migration, racial characteristics, etc and examine whether such factors have anything to do with the 'roots' of insurgency. Of course, the political development during and after the British administration all over Northeast India is one of the most convenient roads to travel to find out and identify the 'roots' of insurgency in the region. The subsequent developments, or those which took place immediately after India's independence, and the indifferent attitude shown by the political leaders of Assam, and the Government of Assam itself, towards the hill tribal people contributed a lot to the problems of insurgency in Northeast India. These and other related issues are being discussed here to find out the contributing factors leading towards the 'roots' of insurgency in Northeast India.

As far as historical development is concerned, be it in the area of administration, political, social and economic, this part of history is a well-known area to all those scholars who have laboriously spent their time, energy and academic pursuits on the North-Eastern Region. Therefore, we need not go into the details of it. The situation is similar, or at least near-similar, to all the tribes or communities in the region. The tribal communities of Northeast India did live an independent life before they came into contact with the British. They were administered independently by their own traditional chiefs and other institutions. This fact is mentioned here purposely, because while explaining one of the 'roots' which gave rise to the problem of insurgency in Northeast India, some such insurgent groups explicitly mentioned this crucial aspect of history as one of the reasons why they wanted to free themselves from the yoke of the Indian State. They invariably go back to their past history and tell the world what they were and how they were administered before the British either annexed or took over the administration of their respective areas. They also made it clear that they want to enjoy the same independent status that their forefathers had enjoyed. This may therefore, be seriously considered as one of the 'roots' of insurgency in Northeast India. Whether such a demand is reasonable, or whether such an arrangement is feasible, or not, it is beyond the purview of this presentation.

In the next stage of administrative development, mention may be made of the British period and its administration over the different areas of Northeast India – hills and plains. To the people of the hills, the British administration was an important milestone which decided many ups and downs in their life –

be it in administrative matters, religious belief, cultural, social and economic, as well as political. The British administration shaped not only the people's life and other activities during that particular period but also their future in different aspects and directions. For example, the Nagas while demanding a sovereign independent State or Nation for themselves, they went on referring to their conditions of independent status before the coming of the British and their acceptance of being conquered and subjugated only by the British and no other forces, before or after that. This has also led them to interpret the Ninth Article or Clause of the famous Hydari Agreement signed between the then Governor of Assam, Sir Akbar Hydari and the Naga leaders in 1947 to mean that after the expiry of the ten year period of the Agreement, the Nagas could assert that they were at liberty to decide their own future, including that of complete separation from the Indian Union. This is an important 'root' in the initial stage of the Naga secessionist or autonomy movement which gave rise to insurgency in Nagaland in the early 1950s. Against this background, it is difficult to deny the fact of the 'influence' of the same 'root' on the secessionist activities and insurgency movements among the Mizos as well as the other tribal and non-tribal communities in almost all areas of Northeast India from the 1960s onward. Therefore, the 'roots' of insurgency that were deeply planted by the Nagas in the 1950s expanded and spread silently to other neighbouring areas of Northeast India.

In the pre-independence period and for few years after India's independence, the tribal communities in Northeast India did not have any psychological and emotional integration with the rest of India. In fact, the integrative forces did not work among the tribal communities immediately after India's independence or even during the time of the Indian struggle for independence from the British rule. The hill tribes of Northeast India cannot be blamed for that. They were not persuaded to get themselves involved in the national freedom struggle. No one took initiative to explain to the hill people the concept of an Indian nation and how the hill tribal people in India's northeast frontier areas could form part of that one nation. This is one of the reasons why they were insulated from the main theatre of national movement which, if things are correctly knitted together, could speak a lot about what were aspired by them on the question of their insulation and indifferent attitudes towards the Indian State. The British authorities were also to a large extent responsible in discouraging the tribal people from taking part in the national freedom movement. The indifference of the tribal people to the Indian national movement, or the failure of that movement to make an impact in the tribal areas in Northeast India, should be considered as a major 'root' of insurgency in the region after the independence of the country.

Even after the independence no serious effort was noticed on the part of the national or provincial leaders to involve the tribal people in Assam in the nation building processes. On the contrary, a section of the Assamese leaders and intellectuals advocated the 'assimilation' of all non-Assamese people in the province of Assam through Assamese language and culture, which ultimately further alienated the tribal people who considered this policy of 'assimilation' as a major threat to their respective cultural identities. The hill state movement started in that background. Therefore, the fear that the tribal identity would be lost as a result of 'assimilation' may be considered as another 'root' of insurgency in Northeast India. It was a grave mistake on the part of the Assamese leaders to have aggressively preached their gospel of 'assimilation' of the tribal communities living within the jurisdiction of the then province of Assam, which was actually created by the British to consist of the traditional Assamese area and some equally traditional tribal areas. Such attempt made by the political leaders of Assam amply demonstrated their short-sightedness, their inability to look beyond their nose and their false pride of superiority complex. To bring home this point, it is worth quoting here what Shri Rohini Kumar Choudhury, a prominent Assamese leader, had to say during the time of the debate in the Constituent Assembly (5-7 September 1949) on the proposed provisions of the Sixth Schedule of the Constitution of India. Shri Rohini Kumar Choudhury was so opposed to the idea of accepting and incorporating the Sixth Schedule into the Indian Constitution and so ethnocentric in his approach towards the hill tribal people of Northeast India that during the course of the Constituent Assembly debates, he had this to say: "We want to assimilate the tribal people. We were not given that opportunity so far. The tribal people, however, much they like (?) had not the opportunity of assimilation." It is thus very clear that there was a serious attempt to assimilate the tribal people of the region into the Assamese society in spite of their opposition to such sinister design by the political leaders of Assam. That is why in his reaction to this kind of intolerant attitude and ethnocentric remark of Shri Rohini Kumar Choudhury, Reverend James Joy Mohon Nichols Roy, a leader of the Khasi-Jaintia Hills, had to strongly defend the proposed provisions of the Sixth Schedule in the Constituent Assembly. He said among other things : "The tribal people should not be allowed to be swallowed up by another culture which is quite different from what they have been used to, and which is considered by them not at all suitable to their society." Therefore, it may not be wrong to say that the intolerant attitude of the Assamese leaders and their sinister attempt to assimilate the tribal people was a serious mistake and its outcome had far reaching consequences in the subsequent years which the political leaders of Assam did not envisage at all. Needless to say, the parochial attitude of the Assamese leaders, which was very clearly reflected in the language policy of the Assam Government, is a very important 'root' of turmoil and mutual distrust among the communities in Assam, which eventually matured into insurgency. It is also equally important to note that the indifferent attitude shown by the other members of the Constituent Assembly from the rest of the country towards the Assamese opposition to the proposed political autonomy to be constitutionally granted to the tribal people in Northeast India, particularly in Assam, had hurt the sentiments of the many tribal leaders of those days and the intolerant opinions of the Assamese leaders continued to haunt the minds and thoughts of the tribal people for many years which actually added to the strengthening of the 'roots' of insurgency in Northeast India.

History tells us clearly and loudly that the seeds of hatred were not sown initially by the tribal people; others were responsible for that. The seeds that were sown by someone were slow to germinate. The roots and tendrils spread out silently beneath the surface long before there was any symptom of sprout or bud. Then suddenly, one fine morning (or should we say, evening), like a springing of a new seed, the soil broke up and a new head of a seed appeared out of the breaking soil. Suddenly, out of nowhere, there was a blaze of colour, an overnight growth; the rebels/insurgents are there and everywhere in the entire Northeast. Thus the fear of assimilation and subjugation of one's own culture and tradition by the more advanced neighbouring people ('more advanced' in terms of language and literature, population, education, economy, and political majority) gave rise to fear and continuous suspicion of the others or outsiders, which ultimately resulted in raising the voice of revolt or armed insurgency, as a means to survive culturally, economically and more important, politically. When the situation had come to the extent of failure to adopt and use constitutional means, the alternative that was left was the use of extra-constitutional means to achieve certain goals, manifesting emancipation – cultural, economic and political. When the voice of democratic or constitutional method of protests and demands seemed to be too feeble to make an impact on the authority which is responsible to provide protection and guarantee development, the militant path seems to have been adopted. Once this method or means is adopted, the definitional meaning of insurgency is also fulfilled.

The support extended to the militants, both through dubious and open means, by other countries bordering Northeast India, is another 'root' which allowed the insurgency in the region to go on and on. The insurgents get and enjoy support from across the borders in different ways and means, like supply of arms and ammunition, places to use as their safe hideouts, training in armed struggle, finance, and all sorts of assistance to keep the struggle alive and kicking all the time. Secondly, it is not only the enemies of India across the borders who come to the help and assistance of the insurgents, there are also other factors that contribute to the cause of the insurgency. The ethnic communities located on the international borders have strong kinship and historical economic linkages with the tribes across the borders. Due to such ethnic affinities, the relationship continues in different ways. The cross-country trade and commerce also strengthens that relationship. The cross-border trade may not necessarily be limited only to essential items, but also include contraband and dangerous goods like arms and ammunition, explosives, drugs, and fake currencies. These items are smuggled from time to time by the insurgents across the borders either for their own use or for sale to other like-minded insurgent groups all over the North-Eastern Region. These clandestine activities help in strengthening the 'roots' of insurgency in the region. Equally important is the porous borders all along the region. The channels to operate against the Indian State are readily available through these borders.

The roots of insurgency in Northeast India may also be linked with the issue or problem of ethnicity and assertion of ethnic identity within the region. The failure of the established authority, that is, the Government of India, to tackle the basic aspects of ethnic question has also been responsible for social, economic and political instability in the region. It is the persistent reluctance of the central government for many decades to openly face the manifestations of the ethnic question in the Northeast that most of the discords began and the same situation continues to exist even today. The different ethnic groups of the region while seeking and trying to redress their problems of deprivation (which arise in various shades and magnitudes) mobilized and organized themselves into different types of pressure groups. Some of them did try to solve their problems within the parameters of the Indian Constitution, but there are many others who did not subscribe to this approach giving the rationale of its hopelessness. They articulated the argument that the Government of India is not aware of the fact that the various ethnic groups in the region have their own history, culture, language, and distinct way of life and that any attempt to ignore this very sensitive aspect of ground reality through assimilation, or political and administrative imposition, is bound to give rise to different forms of aggressive or militant movements. As a matter of fact, the ignorance of the established political authority of the history and culture of the Northeast has already been proved to be true and because of this reason, the 'roots' of insurgency has been strengthened over the years since independence of the country.

Besides the issue of ethnicity or assertion of ethnic identity, the cultural distance of the most of the tribes or communities in Northeast India from the so-called mainstream culture may also be attributed as one of the 'roots' giving rise to insurgency in the region. Most of the ethnic communities in the region found it difficult to appreciate the emerging situation of 'integration' immediately after the independence of the country. This also included the question of centre-periphery relations. The ground reality of the present socio-economic arrangement that provides the push factor towards the extra-constitutional movements of several groups of people in Northeast India mainly centres around two important issues: (a) a policy of national integration with the unresolved nationality question, and (b) the number-oriented decision-making system of the Indian polity.

Finally, there are some instances of disrupted ethnic identity also. For example, the Nagas right from the initial years of India's independence found it hard to locate any common political, cultural or economic ties with the neighbouring non-tribal or other tribal communities to form a common identity. Moreover, the traditional Naga areas were divided between Assam, NEFA, and Manipur. Therefore, the Nagas voiced their demand to remain independent as they could not locate link to the Indian Constitution. The same feeling was expressed in the subsequent years by many other ethnic communities in the region. The hill people also felt let down of their ethnic identity by the passing of the Assam Official Language Act in 1960, which in many respects was directly responsible for the re-organization of the state of Assam. There are still many who remained unsatisfied even with such type of autonomy as conceded by the creation of new states and regional councils and this led them to demand more autonomy, including sovereignty or independent status. It was in this situation that insurgency surfaced in Northeast India.

INTERACTIONS

9

A POSTSCRIPT

—Sarbani Bhattacharjee

The post-lunch session of the Brainstorming Session organized by the Institute of Northeast India Studies, Kolkata, through its Shillong Centre and in collaboration with the Women's College, Shillong, on 26th August 2006, on 'Roots of Insurgency in Northeast India' indeed became a lively free-for-all interactive academic discourse in which the participants freely and frankly expressed themselves on what they considered to be the 'roots' of insurgency in Northeast India. Professor L S Gassah was in the Chair.

Initiating the interaction, Professor Temsula Ao made detailed observation on some of the issues raised by the presenters in the pre-lunch session. Professor Ao said, "During his presentation, Dr Srikanth said that the Nagas claimed that they were never ruled by the Indians before the British came and after India gained Independence they were not going to be ruled by the Indians. But what the Nagas had actually said was that the 'white men' never ruled them and now they were not going to be ruled by the 'black men". This, she felt, was necessary to put the records straight. However, she endorsed

'Dr Srikanth's significant remark that had the Centre agreed to consider the interests of the Nagas when there were signs of unrest among the people and were willing to reconsider their stand on the issue, perhaps a peaceful solution could have emerged long ago.' Referring to Professor L S Gassah's comment, on the presentation of Dr Rakhal Purkayastha in the earlier session, that there has been a constant flow of huge amounts of money into the region for the ostensible purpose of containing insurgency but in actuality much of it was misappropriated by the corrupt officials and politicians, Professor Ao stated, "At one stage intelligence agencies confirmed that if the state machinery so wanted one of the insurgency groups in Nagaland could be completely neutralized. But not only the state and the Centre but also the Army opposed the idea because of the very question of money and perks, which would be stopped once the state ceased to be a 'Disturbed Area'. The subsequent extension of the cease-fire allowed the group to recruit more cadres and arm themselves as well." On the issue of extortion, she opined that "the high idealism of the earlier stages of the movement has been abandoned and instead a culture of indiscriminate harassment of the public by way of demanding exorbitant amounts of money in the name of 'nationalistic' causes continues to be the bane of the people in the region." Professor Ao was of the opinion that 'it was time that the intellectuals of the region need to be involved in the effort to find amicable solutions to the different insurgency problems of the region so that the people can live normal lives and some 'real' developments can take place.' However, she added that in order to achieve this, the Centre also has to reconsider its stand and put 'more heart' into its policies towards the Northeast. Nevertheless, a resolution is possible only when the roots of the problem are identified, Professor Ao emphatically insisted.

Professor Helen Giri narrated her experience as a cultural activist, the experience which she had in course of her interactions with various tribes and communities in various parts of the Northeast. She believed that the roots of insurgency or militancy are to be found in the decline of the traditional social values. The children who are victims of the broken families and those who do not get enough attention of the parents do consider joining the militant groups as a solution to their immediate problem of loneliness. Immorality, drug abuse and the spread of AIDS are also linked to the problem of broken families. There is a sudden affluence for many, and the life-style of the neo rich is different from the rest of the society. She also noted that there are several external factors that are contributing to the growth of militancy. In her opinion, the Khasis were generally proud of their culture and traditions and any misinterpretation of such traditions deeply hurts the Khasi sentiment. She narrated several instances of misinterpretation of the customs and wrong translations of customary terms in various programmes by the organizations like the All India Radio (AIR), and informed that since AIR was a central organization many young people held the central government guilty of distorting the Khasi culture and identity. She also believed that the insensitivity of the government sometimes became responsible for fueling the anger of the youths. A large number of Jaintia villages were included in Karbi Anglong (then called Mikir Hills subdivision) while reorganizing the district and subdvisional boundaries in the

British time. The problem is alive since Independence, and the people in the bordering areas are voters both in Assam and Meghalaya. There had been several assaults and incidences of breakdown of the law and order over the years. A similar situation prevails in the Garo Hills-Assam borders. Since it is an inter-state dispute, it is the responsibility of the central government to step in and find an amicable solution. Professor Giri also shared the information that the Lyngngam area is becoming sensitive every day, as the Lyngngams are divided between the West Khasi Hills and the East Garo Hills districts of Meghalaya. The land alienation is also a serious problem all over the Khasi Hills, particularly in West Khasi Hills. The government has not yet taken any noticeable step towards land reforms, although the problem is becoming more and more serious everyday. She also stated that the rates of school drop-out and unemployment are also very high in West Khasi Hills. She expected that the government should be wise enough to understand that the young people are getting frustrated and the administration should come forward to eliminate the irritants. "While we are discussing the roots of the on-going insurgencies with an objective to resolve these problems, it is better that the government be asked to take appropriate steps to uproot the roots before they lead to the growth of the problem of militancy", Professor Helen Giri observed. In her opinion, 'the indifference of the government to the causes of frustrations and social tensions is an important root of insurgency and militancy in Northeast India'.

Mr Vareipam Muivah opined that the insurgency in the Naga Hills started with the demand for 'Naga independence'. It was a common sentiment for almost all the Nagas. However, in course of time, this has been corrupted in many respects, particularly because of the emergence of new groups and new factions of the original group. Some of the new groups are indulging in extorting money and power-gathering only. These groups have no ideology, or even a community feeling. In his opinion, the 'step-motherly treatment to the Northeast' in the post-independence period by the central government was largely responsible for aggravating the situation. The unemployed and under-employed youths in many parts of the region took up militancy as an alternative to regular employment. This is applicable to all communities in the region as they are the common victims of economic backwardness. In his opinion, the economic backwardness of the region is due to the indifferent attitude and discriminatory polices of the central government towards the Northeast. On the other hand, the lack of infrastructure development was the root cause for frustrations and disappointments among the youths, particularly the educated ones. The government did nothing to tackle the problem of educated unemployment when thousands of educated young people were languishing without opportunities. These young people ultimately provided the manpower for all movements, including militancy and insurgency in the region. He also reiterated that the violation of human rights and excesses committed by the army and the paramilitary forces during various operations against the insurgents had infuriated the people and added to the determination of the youths to fight for their rights. Mr Muivah, however, insisted that the major Naga insurgent groups are still serious about their original demand of independence. The Naga nationalism, and the unity of all Nagas, is still their main concern. The monetary extortion or collecting ransom, as noticed in many parts of the Northeast, is not a significant phenomenon in Nagaland or in the Naga areas of Manipur and Assam, since the Naga groups whenever they collect money they do it publicly as a tax or contribution to the Naga cause and they issue formal receipts on behalf of their organizations.

Agreeing with Mr Muivah that all insurgents are not extortionists, Mrs Julie Hazarika said: "There are many faces of terrorism in our region today. Some youths with ideological aspirations might have begun the movements with honest intentions of formulating a better society, but the fall out may be spurious. The spurious groups are found to harass the public. Such groups posing as terrorists indulge in unlawful activities such as extortion, abduction, kidnapping of minors - all for pure monetary gains. My question is how do we with all the vulnerability of our conditions ensconced in our comfortable life style handle the situation ? The brainstorming session today is a laudable attempt to face the problem squarely, but follow up in the shape of further discussion and addressing wider forum is the call of the hour. Our concern must be taken to the streets if we are to uproot the menace. Let us not be terrorized, and let us foil all the attempts at destabilization by anti-national elements." She was emphatic that extortion is as serious a menace as insurgency or terrorism, and the intellectuals may like to bring this problem within the scope of the discourse.

Mrs Hazarika's intervention generated a comprehensive discussion on the extortionist dimension of insurgency or militancy in Northeast India. Some of the participants referred to media reports and other sources informing how the extortionists used the names of militants or insurgents, like 'liberation tigers', 'army', etc, in their demand notes or demanded ransom after abductions in such names. It was also observed that the extortionists are only taking the advantage of the prevalent insurgent situation in the region. However, describing the extortionists as pseudo-insurgents or pseudo-terrorists, Professor J B Bhattacharjee argued that a clear line should be drawn between 'insurgency' and 'extortion'. According to him, the extortionists are simple criminals and should be dealt with by the state accordingly. In no way, they should be confused with the insurgents or the militants. Dr Rakhal Purkayastha wanted that the possibility of a politician-terrorist nexus to ensure the flow of money from the centre should also be examined. Professor Ao drew attention to media reports which revealed that in several instances the extortionists had indulged in abduction and kidnapping in the name of insurgents and militants for the simple purpose of demanding and collecting ransom. These groups have nothing to do with any of the on-going movements in the region. The root of all problems, according Professor Ao, is the rampant corruption which has infringed in every aspect of human life and activity in the region. Professor Helen Giri, Mr Vareipam Muivah, Mr Surajit Sen and Mr Joydeep Bhattacharjee observed that these extortionist groups might consist of the unemployed youths who could not find any other avenues for earning their livelihood. However, it was felt that the possibility of some of the insurgent or terrorist groups collecting money from the wealthy persons and families to finance their activities and to maintain themselves cannot be ruled out. Mrs Esther Rimai suggested that to understand the roots of insurgency or militancy or the extortionist activities the historical background of the various groups involved in such activities should be thoroughly studied, because only such studies will bring out why each particular group originated, and what are its objectives and purposes. Ms Jayati Bhattacharjee reiterated, what she said in her presentation, that insurgency or terrorism or extortions – all these are rooted in economic backwardness, unemployment problem and the lack of opportunities for decent way of earning. Once the problem of economic and infrastructural backwardness is removed the opportunities will present themselves and all other concomitant menaces will also disappear, she maintained. The Chairman, Professor L S Gassah described insurgency as 'the most flourishing industry in the unorganized sector' in Northeast India today. In his opinion, the insurgents or terrorists or extortionists – all are indulging in extortions in one form or other. The difference is that while the insurgents or terrorists or leaders of other movements may be collecting money partly for the programme and partly for themselves, the extortionists are doing it for themselves only. Nevertheless, the extortionists are only taking the advantage of a lawless situation which has been created by none other than the insurgents and the militants, because everything in the region today goes in the name of insurgency. The insurgency and money do go together. The state governments are asking for more money from the centre in the name of fighting or motivating the insurgents, or rehabilitating the surrendered militants. All the officers who handle the 'special funds' may not be equally honest to spend the entire amount for the cause. Similarly, escalation on delayed projects is considered justified on ground of insurgency. Generally, any project in the Northeast is hardly completed in time. It is not known whether the additional amounts of money sanctioned on ground of escalation would go only to the contractor as the genuinely enhanced project cost or these are shared with the officials. Again, the government employees in some parts of the region are enjoying 'disturbed area' or 'special duty' allowances. The employees in some central organizations and public sector undertakings from outside the region are also entitled to 'home posting' after having served in the Northeast for three years. The continuation of such allowances depends on the endurance of the 'disturbed' conditions or 'special' situation in the region. Therefore, there are too many 'nexuses' and 'incentives', Professor Gassah felt, to allow the insurgency to continue. Unless, all the vested interests are identified and tackled category-wise the insurgency cannot be up-rooted, he observed.

Mr Joydeep Bhattacharjee reiterated his earlier point that the retarded nation-building processes, particularly the segregationist policies, are responsible for the lack of national integration in the region, and as a result, a psychological distance persists between the rest of India and the local communities in Northeast India. On the other hand, Ms Sunanda Bhattacharya insisted that the Northeast alone is not responsible for the lack of integration, because the rest of India is also guilty of not treating the Northeast on terms of equality. According to her, "Discrimination has been an integral part of human civilization. Discrimination on grounds of race, colour, and religion and so on has always been there in human society. What we often forget is that such discrimination leads to a number of social problems and gives birth to conflicts. The north-eastern region too had to face discrimination and alienation. The step-motherly treatment faced by the region has been responsible for the rise of discontentment among the people of the region, adding fuel to already existing problems." She also referred to some instances which show that the people in the mainland considered those in the Northeast as different. She said, "Often students going out of the region have to face discrimination. I remember an incident, where one of my friends from Delhi, once told me that the people from the north-eastern region are given the name 'Chini' for they possess chunky eyes. The remark made by the friend was illuminating in the sense that it threw a lot of light on the attitude of the rest of India towards the region, where we find the whole region with its different cultures and languages reduced to one single term, i.e. 'chini'." These two interventions made the discussion livelier. A number of other speakers also cited examples of how the people from this region are treated as strangers in other parts of the country, including how 'Shillong' is confused with 'Cylone'.

However, Professor L S Gassah, Professor J B Bhattacharjee, Professor Temsula Ao, Professor Helen Giri, Dr Rakhal Purkayastha, Mr Vareipam Muivah, Mr Surajit Sen and others took the discussion on problem of integration to its academic height when they referred to the concepts like 'unity in diversity' which historically prevailed all over the Indian subcontinent, the evidences of 'pan-Indian culture continuum' in parts of the Northeast since early times, the fact of diversity not only in the context of the subcontinent but even within the Northeast, and the debates on 'integration versus assimilation'. The speakers insisted that what our cultural policy should aim at is not 'assimilation' but 'integration'. This country was never unicultural and the multiplicity of cultures is its beauty. They also contested the 'mainstream theory' and argued that every stream of culture in the country is 'a main stream' and should be valued and respected accordingly. The Indian national movement recognized this cultural diversity of the subcontinent through all-India cultural conferences, which were organized along with the annual sessions of the Indian National Congress, and the concepts of regional languages, linguistic provinces, secularism, etc were emphasized in course of that historic movement. In fact, the 'Indian Nation' emerged through the Indian National Movement, which was one of the world's largest and the longest anti-colonial struggles. These principles were consciously enshrined in the Constitution of India that was framed by the national leaders, who were drawn from every part of the country and who were products of the Indian National Movement. The idea was to convince the people that they can be the integral parts of the great Indian nation without losing their respective cultural and linguistic identities and to ensure the endurance of the spirit of the Indian national movement. A large number of languages were listed in the relevant schedule of the constitution, which are supposed to be equal in status. English was to continue as the official and the link language at the national level till such time as it could be replaced by Hindi. In Northeast India, English is the link language. It is also the official language for most of the states and the medium of education in most of the institutions. Hindi has only a marginal impact in this region. The social tensions and a process of disintegration commenced with the aggressive attitude of the fanatics, who enjoyed political support, for imposing Assamese and Hindi. A sense of insecurity for the ethnic and cultural identities, and the resultant inhospitable attitude of the locals towards the outsiders, originated from that point of time. The cultural and linguistic policies of the centre and the states are, therefore, among the important roots of insurgency and militancy in Northeast India. 'Integration is desirable, but not assimilation' was the dominant tune.

The interaction delved in-depth into yet another important area when Professor Helen Giri raised the question of the role of education in the nation-building processes vis-à-vis the educated youths being drawn to militancy or pseudo-militancy for financial extortions. The role of education is more or less an unfamiliar issue in the discourses on insurgency, as it would be evident from the large volumes of published literature on the subject. Nevertheless, the participants in this brain-storming session being almost all of them from the academics (more precisely, the teachers), Professor Giri's intervention, as it was expected, provided a lively insight for an in-house deliberation or self-introspection by the professionals of education without losing the basic tenor of the session. To put in a nutshell what transpired in response to the question, the participants observed that the stresses and strains of time and circumstances have effected fundamental changes in the very objective and purpose of education in India as a whole and the Northeast in particular. The classical spirit of education in relation to character-building or man-making - moral and value education - has been undergoing significant changes in last fifty years. The nation-building and national or human integration required emphasis on moral and value education and the wisdom of the traditional disciplines or classical subjects, but those subjects could not hold water in the context of the emerging demand for marketability or commoditization. Therefore, education today aims at arming the youths to earn their livelihood, and accordingly, the job-oriented and professional courses are globally more emphasized. The line between education and training has been gradually obliterated and the training institutes are re-designated as universities. The traditional disciplines of knowledge and wisdom are getting relegated, while the marketability of the products (i.e. graduates) is considered more important in designing the courses and programmes. The research and development (R&D), industry-institution linkages, and quality circles have become key-words in educational management, and the entire process of education is dominated by the market forces. The Northeast has been too slow in responding to the wind of change, despite its remarkable progress in literacy and formal education, including higher education, since independence. The curriculum here continued to be a colonial hangover of conventional combinations in the basic disciplines. Nothing spectacular happened towards modernization, commercialization and professionalization of the courses. On the other hand, the affluent parents started to send their children, particularly after plus-two stage, to Bangalore, Pune and other places, partly for education in technical and professional courses and partly to escape the ramifications of disturbed conditions in the region. More meritorious students of the region were generally among those who went to study outside the region. The institutions within the region did not show much enthusiasm to catch up the thrill of new courses mainly due to the financial constraints, and they were in many cases required only to look after the left over of the talents. In the process, the general degree colleges suffered stagnation and deterioration due to poor funding and lack of infrastructure. Most of the universities in the region were slow in up-dating the curriculum even in conventional subjects, and the new generation of students was more interested in getting the degrees than in education. The attendance in the colleges fell in many cases, and the private tuitions became a profitable enterprise in some areas. In some cases it was also rumoured that the tuition lobby was opposing the revision of syllabus. In a highly charged situation under fear of terrorist attacks, it became at a point of time a serious challenge to maintain discipline in some of the educational institutions. However, more important than all these was the fact of demoralization of the youths due to unemployment and lack of opportunities. The fact that the elder youths, despite education and possessing degrees, were suffering frustration and disappointment due to unemployment spontaneously caused disill-usionment among the students in colleges and high schools. This influenced the attitude of the students towards education, and the rate of drop-outs increased significantly. The drop-outs joining the ranks of the militants and extortionists were also rumoured. The participants, therefore, felt that the education might not have directly played any role in militancy or insurgency, but it was itself a victim of the overall dismal conditions that prevailed in the region for a long time. However, education created a large pool of unemployed youths which became handy for the insurgency and militancy to draw their cadres. The role of education was further emphasized by Mr Debasish Chowdhury, Principal, Women's College, who, while proposing the vote of thanks, elaborated on the need to provide quality education in the era of globalization when the life is so competitive and called upon all concerned for a change of attitude to facilitate the modernization of courses for matching the real life challenges of the twenty-first century.

On the main issues raised in various presentations in the pre-lunch session, namely, the historical and geographical factors, failure of the central government to find out amicable solutions to the problem of insurgency when insurgency broke out first in the Naga Hills and then in Mizo Hills and Manipur, the excesses committed by the administration and army, the violation of human rights, alienation and deprivation of the ethnic and linguistic minorities due to wrong policies of the state governments and the absolute reliance of the central government on the state governments in resolving the problems of the minorities within the states, the role of the neighbouring countries in promoting insurgency and militancy in the region as part of their policy to destabilize and weaken the Indian state, indifference of the central government towards the development of the Northeast, economic backwardness of the region, unemployment and lack of opportunities for the youths, rampant corruptions at various levels, the growth of regionalism, etc, there was no disagreement with the presenters. On the contrary, the discussants strengthened the arguments of the presenters with examples and analyses. The single common root that was emphasized most is the indifferent attitude of the central government towards the Northeast, which in turn created economic and infrastructural backwardness of the region, unemployment and lack of opportunities for the youths, frustrations and disappointments, a sense of deprivation in the masses, ethnic discrimination, a feeling of insecurity and threat to cultural identity among the minorities, and many other related problems.

The position that emerged very clearly in course of the interactions is that there is nothing like a north-eastern insurgency and that all the disturbances and turmoil happening in the region are not necessarily insurgencies. Only the Naga and the Meitei movements, and the Mizo movement at a point of time, can be described as genuine insurgencies in strict sense of the term, though in course of time the majority in those ethnic communities might have reconciled themselves with the Indian state and small segments are still pursuing the original demands. The second group, sometimes confused with the insurgents, is the militants, who emerged from the demands for regional autonomy for their respective ethnic communities within the Indian state. When the democratic political movements on those demands failed to impress the central government, the radical sections from within the movements opted for militancy and sometimes assumed anti-Indian postures by attacking the administration and the army. The Bodo, Karbi, Dimasa, Kuki, Garo, Bru or Riang or Chakma militant groups fall within this category. The radical section within the Assam Movement originally demanded political and economic autonomy for Assam and eventually formed ULFA to declare war against the Indian state. It is an insurgency only since then. There is also a third category where handfuls of individuals formed armed groups and indulged in kidnapping and abductions for the purpose of monetary extortions, but gave themselves militants' names. They are not genuine insurgents or militants. The genuine insurgent and militant groups are also fighting for the cause of their own ethnic communities only and their universe is limited to the respective ethnic areas. The ethnic interests are sometimes conflicting and clash with each other. There is hardly any coordination or common cause between the groups. The root cause for the rise of each group is different, and each one stands for its own community interests. No one stands for the Northeast as a whole. Therefore, there is nothing like a north-eastern insurgency. Each one is called by its own name, e.g. 'Naga insurgency', 'Meitei insurgency', 'Bodo militancy', 'Dimasa militancy', and the like, and the roots of each insurgency or militancy has to be identified separately. The demands of each group are limited to its own ethnic community or the ethnic area. There is no demand or movement for the development of the Northeast as a region. Therefore, it is ethnicity or 'localism', and not 'regionalism'.

The speakers also observed that the only common factor often cited by most of the groups is the economic backwardness of the Northeast, but even a united democratic movement for the development of the entire region is yet to be seen. The non-militant agitations like 'road blockade' or 'bund' or 'boycott" of offices or institutions are limited to states or parts of states. No one heard of a 'Northeast bund' or an agitation for the development of the entire Northeast. The discussion moved further to consider in what sense is the Northeast a region. The position that emerged promptly is the problem of conceptualizing Northeast India as a 'historical region' for the purpose of a 'regional history', as different from a contemporary administrative division or an economic zone for the purpose of infrastructure development. A region in history generally represents certain common geographical and ethno-cultural features, a common heritage, and the experience of common historical processes in terms of social and polity formations. Besides geographical and environ-mental variations, the Northeast is well known for its ethnic, linguistic and cultural diversities. It did not experience one common regional state at any point of time in history. On the contrary, the tribal communities zealously guarded their ethnic boundaries as per the settlement patterns and were governed by their respective traditional institutions, while the monarchies which emerged in the plains areas exhausted themselves in mutual conflicts and warfare before the British colonized the region. The Burmese invasion that preceded the British intervention had exposed the weaknesses of the local monarchies which were actually on decline. The British rule had for the first time provided a common political authority when the Northeast was made a part of the British Indian colonial state. As some speakers had already pointed out, the regionalization of the Northeast was not possible in that period also due to the segregating policies of the colonial rulers, on the one hand, and the attitude of the local tribes and communities towards each other, on the other hand. The 'national integration' that is being discussed is certainly much larger an issue than the 'regional integration' which is also yet to be achieved in the Northeast. The slogans like 'seven sisters' do not mean much once one faces the hard facts. The boundary disputes between the states is already an annoyingly persistent ground reality, while the current trend of setting up most of the regional offices and institutions in Guwahati and Shillong is alienating the other areas. The speakers insisted that, since 'charity begins at home', the 'regional integration' should be a step towards the 'national integration' and this will require a charge of heart on the part of the dominant elite within the region. It was further insisted that the intellectuals of the region should play a role in bringing the people together and accelerating the process of integration.

The interactive session ended with a broad consensus on the basic roots of insurgencies and militancies in Northeast India, although the participants repeatedly made it clear that these are not the last words and many more rounds of discourses would be necessary to reach the closest approximation of the ground realities. In his concluding remarks, the Chairman, Professor L S Gassah, complemented the Institute of Northeast India Studies for its laudable initiative in organizing this brainstorming session of the academics and the researchers on 'Roots of Insurgency in Northeast India'. He referred to the attempts of the government from time to time to resolve the problem of insurgency and militancy by political, administrative and military means, but the problem has been continuing for almost fifty years. On the other hand, the strong-arm tactics of the authorities sometimes complicated the situation further and eventually boomerang into breeding new problems. They tried to solve the problem without understanding the causes of the problem, and this explains why the problem continues for such a long time. The identification of the roots or causes requires sustained research and analysis, which the academia of the region should take up in the spirit of a social commitment. This brainstorming session is, therefore, a new beginning of an old journey for conflict resolution in Northeast India and it should be followed up by more sessions. "The insurgency must end, but it is possible only when its roots are identified and uprooted", Professor Gassah concluded.

APPENDIX

Appendix

OUR PARTICIPANTS

Professor J B Bhattacharjee, Chairman, Institute of Northeast India Studies, 'Barak', 13/A Udayan Abasan, Udayrajpur, Madhyamgram, Kolkata – 700129

Professor L S Gassah, Department of Political Science, North-Eastern Hill University, Shillong – 793022

Professor (Mrs) Temsula Ao, Dean, School of Humanities & Education, North-Eastern Hill University, Shillong – 793022

Professor (Mrs) Helen Giri, Chairperson, Babu Jeebon Roy Academy of Music and Dance, Umsoshun, Shillong – 793002

Dr (Mrs) Bhaswati Lahiri, Lecturer (Selection Grade) in Bengali, Lady Keane College, Shillong – 793001

Dr Binayak Dutta, Lecturer in History, St Edmund's College, Shillong - 793003

Dr Rakhal Purkayastha, Lecturer (Selection Grade) in Political Science, St Anthony's College, Shillong – 793003

Mr Debasish Chowdhury, Principal, Women's College, Shillong – 793003

Mr Vareipam Muivah, Lecturer in Political Science, Women's College, Shillong – 793003

Mr Surajit Sen, Lecturer in English, Women's College, Shillong – 793003

Dr (Ms) Alicia Gatpoh, Lecturer in History, Raid Laban College, Shillong – 793004

Mr Joydeep Bhattacharjee, Correspondent, The Shillong Times, Shillong – 793004

Dr Y N Karna, Head, Department of Sociology, Women's College, Shillong – 793003

Ms Chongboi Lhouvum, Lecturer in Sociology, Women's College, Shillong – 793003

Ms Mitali Bhattacharjee, Lecturer in English, Women's College, Shillong – 793003

Ms Sunanda Bhattacharya, Lecturer in English, Women's College, Shillong – 793003

Dr H Srikanth, Reader in Political Science, North-Eastern Hill University, Shillong – 73022

Dr (Mrs) Mala Ranganathan, Reader in English, North-Eastern Hill University, Shillong – 793022

Mrs Angira Kar, Lecturer in History, Women's College, Shillong – 793003

Mrs Julie Hazarika, Head, Department of English, Women's College, Shillong - 793003

Mrs Ameeta Roy, Lecturer in History, Women' College, Shillong – 793003

Mrs Meena Dev Sharma, Lecturer in Assamese, Women's College, Shillong – 793003

Mrs K Rita Devi, Lecturer in English, Women's College, Shillong – 793003

Mrs Nila Dutta, Lecturer in Sociology, Women's College, Shillong – 793003

Ms Phioshua Kharkonger, Head, Department of History, Women's College, Shillong – 793003

Mrs Esther Rimai, Lecturer in Education, Women's College, Shillong – 793003

Mrs Ruma Das, Head, Department of Political Science, Women's College, Shillong – 93003

Mrs Sanu Mukherjee, Head, Department of Philosophy, Women's College, Shillong – 793003

Dr (Ms) Sumana Paul, Head, Department of Education, Women's College, Shillong – 793003

Dr (Mrs) Sonali Roy Paul, Lecturer in Education, Women's College, Shillong – 793003

Mrs Haimanti Choudhury, Lecturer in Economics, Women's College, Shillong – 793003

Mrs Devjani Kar, Lecturer in Economics, Women's College, Shillong – 793003

Ms Sarbani Bhattacharjee, Lecturer in History, Bissau College, Shillong – 793003

Ms Sangeeta Dasgupta, Lecturer in Economics, Women's College, Shillong – 793003

Ms Jayati Bhattacharjee, Lecturer in History, Women's College, Shillong - 793003

SELECT BIBLIOGRAPHY

All India People's Resistance Forum, *Symphony of Freedom: Papers on Nationality Question,* Hyderabad, 1996.

Ashok Kr Roy & B J Deb (ed), *Insurgency and Human Rights in North East India,* New Delhi, 2007.

Ashok Kr Roy & S K Agnihotri (ed), *Terrorism and Peace Initiatives in North East India,* New Delhi, 2006.

Ajay Roy, *The Boro Imbroglio,* Guwahati, 2002.

B B Kumar (ed), *Reorganization of North East India,* New Delhi, 1996.

Bhushan Chandra, *Terrorism and Separatism in North East India,* New Delhi, 2004.

B Datta Ray (ed), *Tribal Identity and Terrsism in North East India,* New Delhi, 1981.

B Pakem (ed), *Insurgency in North East India,* New Delhi, 1997.

Chirom Ranjit, *Unrest in Manipur,* Imphal, 2004.

C. Joshua Thomas (ed), *Polity and Economy: Agenda for Contemporary North East India,* New Delhi, 2005.

C Joshua Thomas, R Gopal Krishan & R K Rajan Singh, *Constraints in Development of Manipur,* Imphal, 2001.

Govt. of India, *Annual Report 2004-05,* Ministry of Home Affairs, New Delhi.

H K Barpujari, *North East India–Problems, Policies and Prospects,* Guwahati, 1998.

Imdad Hussain (ed), *The Guwahati Declaration and the Road to Peace in Assam,* New Delhi, 2005.

J B Bhattacharjee (ed), *Social Tensions in North East India,* Culcutta, 1982.

J B Bhattacharjee, *Negotiating Insurgency and Cross-Border Terrorism: Challenges of Peace and Transformation in Asia in 21st Century,* General Presidential Address, Indian Conress for Asian and Pacific Studies, Fifth Conference, Jammu, November, 8-10, 2000.

Lakshmi Krishnamurti, R Swaminathan, Gert W. Kueck (ed), *Responding to Terrorism: Dilemmas of Democratic & Developing Soceities,* Madras, 2003.

Lt. Gen. N.S. Narahari, *Security Threats to North East India: The Socio-Ethnic Tensions,* New Delhi, 2002.

Lucy Zehol, *Ethnicity in Manipur,* New Delhi, 1998.

Maj. Gen. Virinder Uberoy, *Combating Terrorism,* New Delhi, 1992.

M Horam, *Naga Insurgency,* New Delhi, 1998.

M Horam (ed), *The Rising Manipur,* New Delhi, 2001.

M N Karna (ed), *Social Movements in North East India,* New Delhi, 1998.

Nameirakpam Bisheshor, *Battle of Waterloo 1987,* Imphal, 1987.

Niru Hazarika, *Ethnic Autonomy Question in North East India,* Guwahat, 1999.

N Joykumar Singh, *Revolutionary Movements in Manipur,* New Delhi, 2005.

N Joykumar Singh, *Social Movements in Manipur,* New Delhi, 1992.

N Lokendra Singh, *Unquiet Valley,* New Delhi, 1998.

Phanjouban Tarapot, *Insurgency Movement in North Eastern India,* New Delhi, 1993.

Phanjoubam Tarapot, *Bleeding Manipur*, New Delhi, 2004.

R P Anand, *South Asia: In Search of a Regional Identity*, New Delhi, 1991.

R Horam, *The Genesis of Naga Political Movement*, New Delhi, 1998.

R Vashum, *Nagas' Right to Self-Determination*, New Delhi, 2000.

Sanjoy Hazarika, *Strangers of the Mist: Tales of War and Peace from India's Northeast*, New Delhi, 1995.

Sajal Nag, *Contesting Marginalities: Ethnicity, Insurgency and Subnationalism in North East India*, New Delhi, 2002.

Sanjib Baruah, *India Against Itself–Assam and the Politics of Nationality*, New Delhi, 1999.

S C Sharma, *Insurgency or Ethnic Conflict*, New Delhi, 2000.

S K Agnihotri & B Datta Ray (ed), *Perspectives of Security and Development in North East India*, New Delhi, 2005.

S K Chaube, *Hill Politics in North East India*, Culcutta, 1974.

Susheela Bhan, *Terrorism: An Annotated Bibliography*, New Delhi, 1989.

Udoyan Misra, *Periphery Strikes Back*, New Delhi, 1998.

V K Anand, *Insurgency and Counter Insurgency: A Study of Modern Guerilla Warfare*, New Delhi, 1981.

V K Nuh, *Struggle for Identity in North East India*, Guwahati, 2001.

V K Nuh, *My Native Country – The Land of the Nagas*, Guwahati, 2000.

V K Sarin, *India's North East in Flames*, New Delhi, 1979.

Y D Gundevia, *War and Peace in Nagaland*, New Delhi, 1975.

INDEX